YORK NO'

General Editors: Profe
of Stirling) & Professo
University of Beirut)

C000039807

William Shakespeare

LOVE'S LABOUR'S LOST

Notes by John Saunders

MA (CAMBRIDGE) B PHIL (OXFORD)
Lecturer in English Literature
University of Newcastle upon Tyne

LONGMAN
YORK PRESS

YORK PRESS
Immeuble Esseily, Place Riad Solh, Beirut.

LONGMAN GROUP LIMITED
London
*Associated companies, branches and representatives
throughout the world*

First published 1980
ISBN 0 582 78220 1
Printed in Hong Kong by
Sing Cheong Printing Co Ltd

Contents

Part 1: Introduction   *page* 5

Shakespeare the man   5
Shakespeare and the theatre   6
Shakespeare and the age   9
A note on the text   11

Part 2: Summaries   12

A general summary   12
Detailed summaries   13

Part 3: Commentary   58

The title   58
The sources   58
Critical history   59
The characters   61
Plot and structure   65
Language   67
The play   69

Part 4: Hints for study   71

Approaching the play   71
Selecting quotations   72
Topics for study   73
Essay questions   74
Writing an essay   75

Part 5: Suggestions for further reading   78

The author of these notes   80

Part 1

Introduction

Shakespeare the man

We know almost nothing of Shakespeare's early life except that he was baptised at Holy Trinity Church, Stratford-upon-Avon, on 26 April 1564, and that he married Ann Hathaway at the end of 1582. Since his father, a glove-maker and business man of some standing in the town, had connections with the local grammar school, it is reasonable to assume that Shakespeare attended there and received the Latin-based education of the day. Records show that his father's fortunes declined after about 1577, and Shakespeare may have had to leave school early. Apart from his marriage to Ann, the birth of a daughter in May 1583 and of twins the following year, we know nothing of him until 1592, when it seems he was already established in London as an actor and playwright. In the intervening years we may, if we wish, imagine him poaching deer on the estate of Sir Thomas Lucy, as legend has it, or teaching as a country schoolmaster, or more probably joining a provincial theatrical company and so finding his way to the capital in the late 1580s.

From town records and legal documents we know that by the late 1590s he was wealthy enough to buy property, including New Place, a large house in Stratford. His family probably remained in the town, and Hamnet, his only son, died there in 1596. Shakespeare retired to spend his last years in Stratford and on 25 April 1616 he was buried in the church where he had been baptised fifty-two years before.

To add some colour to the factual record, Shakespeare's works are often pressed for biographical information. In 1593 he published a long poem *Venus and Adonis* and dedicated it to the Earl of Southampton. The following year another poem, *The Rape of Lucrece*, probably written while the theatres were closed because of the plague, was also dedicated to Southampton. We know a good deal about the Earl, who was ten years younger than the poet, but nothing of any connection between them beyond these dedications. Shakespeare's sonnets were not printed until 1609, though most of them appear to date from the 1590s, and attempts to see the dedicatee, 'Mr W. H.', as Southampton are unconvincing. Indeed the dedication may be the publisher's rather than the author's, and centuries of scholarship have been unable to identify either Mr W. H., or the noble youth to whom the bulk of the sonnets are addressed, or the 'Dark Lady' who appears in some of the later ones. These probably coincide in date with *Love's Labour's Lost* and Berowne's Rosaline has the same colouring and is defended in the same terms as the mistress of whom Shakespeare writes in sonnet 132:

> Then will I swear beauty herself is black,
> And all they foul that thy complexion lack.

Yet the sonnet and the sonnet sequence were highly artificial forms and Shakespeare the private individual is no more visible here than in the plays. It is because he wrote the plays that Shakespeare the man continues to fascinate us.

Shakespeare and the theatre

The company with which Shakespeare is particularly associated was the Lord Chamberlain's Men until 1603 when James I, the new king, became their patron and as the recognised leaders in their profession they became known as the King's Men. All Shakespeare's plays were written with the actors of this company in mind and to demonstrate their skills. To take an example, the change in the nature of the clowns' roles after 1599 is generally explained by the fact that Will Kempe, who specialised in acrobatic comedy, was succeeded in that year by Robert Armin, a 'wise fool' noted for his singing. Shakespeare himself was both writer and actor, and as late as 1603 he is listed as one of the company acting in Ben Jonson's *Sejanus his Fall*. He was also a ten per cent shareholder when the Globe theatre was erected in 1599.

Although Shakespeare's plays were performed in a number of London theatres he is associated above all with the Globe until one of his plays literally brought the house down. In 1613 cannon used in a performance of *Henry VIII* set fire to the thatched roof and the building was destroyed. We have no details of the dimensions of the theatre but surviving records for other houses give us the main features of an Elizabethan theatre. Three galleries ran round an open courtyard into which the stage projected more than twenty feet, so that the 'groundlings', those members of the audience who paid for standing room only, surrounded it on three sides. Wealthier patrons occupied the galleries and the total audience may have been as many as three thousand. The stage itself was head-high, to allow for trap-doors, and covered by a canopy. At the back was the 'tiring house' where the actors changed and from which they made their entrances. Another gallery along the front of the tiring house provided a raised area when needed, as for the balcony scene in *Romeo and Juliet*. When in Act IV Scene 3 of our play Berowne says 'Like a demi-god here sit I in the sky' no doubt he was hidden there, or in a tree attached to it.

The open stage demanded the kind of 'theatre-in-the-round' which has re-emerged only in the last few decades. An actor might be closer to the audience than to his fellow actors at the back of the stage, so that the many soliloquies and asides found in Shakespeare's plays were a natural consequence of the physical situation. The absence of a front curtain meant that the action probably flowed without interruption and elaborate fixed scenery was not possible, though there were more 'props' and special effects than was once believed. Surviving inventories show that in 1598 one of the rival companies possessed a 'tree of golden apples', two 'moss banks', and a 'chain of dragons', and presumably

THE GLOBE PLAYHOUSE

The theatre, originally built by James Burbage in 1576, was made of wood (Burbage had been trained as a carpenter). It was situated to the north of the River Thames on Shoreditch in Finsbury Fields. There was trouble with the lease of the land, and so the theatre was dismantled in 1598, and reconstructed 'in another forme' on the south side of the Thames as the Globe. Its sign is thought to have been a figure of the Greek hero Hercules carrying the globe. It was built in six months, its galleries being roofed with thatch. This caught fire in 1613 when some smouldering wadding, from a cannon used in a performance of Shakespeare's *Henry VIII*, lodged in it. The theatre was burnt down, and when it was rebuilt again on the old foundations, the galleries were roofed with tiles.

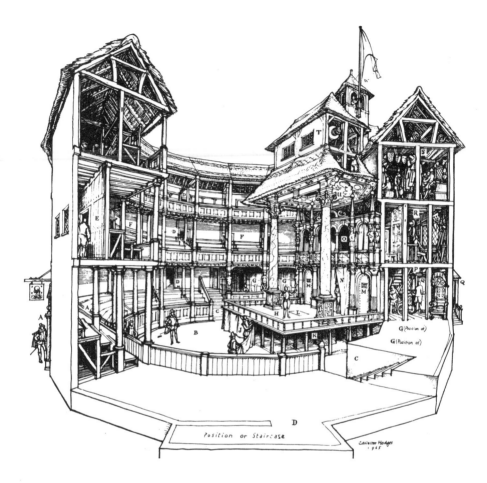

A CONJECTURAL RECONSTRUCTION OF THE INTERIOR OF THE GLOBE PLAYHOUSE

AA Main entrance
 B The Yard
CC Entrances to lowest gallery
 D Entrance to staircase and upper galleries
 E Corridor serving the different sections of the middle gallery
 F Middle gallery ('Twopenny Rooms')
 G 'Gentlemen's Rooms' or Lords' Rooms'
 H The stage
 J The hanging being put up round the stage
 K The 'Hell' under the stage
 L The stage trap, leading down to the Hell
MM Stage doors

N Curtained 'place behind the stage'
O Gallery above the stage, used as required sometimes by musicians, sometimes by spectators, and often as part of the play
P Back-stage area (the tiring-house)
Q Tiring-house door
R Dressing-rooms
S Wardrobe and storage
T The hut housing the machine for lowering enthroned gods, etc., to the stage
U The 'Heavens'
W Hoisting the playhouse flag

the Lord Chamberlain's Men were not to be outdone in this department.

Since women were not allowed on the public stage, all female roles were played by boys. No doubt this was a limitation, but Shakespeare's plays still give us some of the world's most famous love stories. Suggestions that a highly stylised kind of acting must have been used by men and boys alike probably underestimate the ability of the specially trained boy actors. The acting may have differed from what we know today, but the relatively intimate nature of the theatre and the range of Shakespeare's verse point to something no less powerful. In Richard Burbage the company possessed the leading actor of his day and the creator of most of Shakespeare's tragic heroes. Hamlet's advice to the players shows that by 1601 Burbage and his fellows were not content to bawl the lines:

> Nor do not saw the air too much with your hand, thus; but use all gently: for in the very torrent, tempest, and—as I may say—whirlwind of passion, you must acquire and beget a temperance, that may give it smoothness.
>
> (*Hamlet*, III.2.4–9)

In 1608 the King's Men took a second theatre at Blackfriars and played the winter season there; again Shakespeare was one of the seven shareholders. The building was much smaller than the Globe, the audience more select, and indoor lighting was required. Some of the changes in Shakespeare's late romances such as *The Tempest* and *The Winter's Tale* may be explained by the move, although the company continued to use the Globe as well. The new fashion for the Court Masque with elaborate machinery and effects, developed by the architect Inigo Jones (1573–1652), must have counted for something too.

The theatre had come a long way from the comedies, moralities and chronicle plays which held the stage when Shakespeare arrived in London and Christopher Marlowe (1564–93) was the leading dramatist of the time. Yet the conventions established in those early years lie behind all Shakespeare's work.

Shakespeare and the age

Though the plays may not give us Shakespeare the man they do give us the times in which he lived. He was the most successful of dramatists because his plays held the mirror up to a nature which his contemporaries recognised and shared. The playhouse and the world interpenetrated, and the actors were not confined to the public stages but invited to perform at court. The life of the nobility involved considerable ceremony, and masques and pageants like those in the final act of our play would form part of the programme when the Queen was entertained.

The great houses sometimes had their own troupes of players, usually made up of boy-choristers, catering for a sophisticated audience who had studied the classical authors and could write verses themselves. The 'university wits', as the playwrights who wrote for the aristocracy were sometimes known, affected to despise the popular theatre, but writers such as Shakespeare were quick to profit from their example. Parallels have often been drawn between his early comedies and the plays of John Lyly (*c*.1554–1606), with their elegant yet easy combination of wit and argument, song and satire. In *Endimion, The Man in the Moon* (1591) Sir Tophas, 'a foolish braggart', and his page Epiton may remind us of Armado and Moth in *Love's Labour's Lost*, and the prologue to the same play defends the mixed mode which we associate with Shakespeare above all. Lyly's more famous prose work *Euphues: The Anatomy of Wit* (1578) is concerned with the conflict between wit and true wisdom, self-love and experience, which provides some of Shakespeare's favourite themes, both in *Love's Labour's Lost* and later.

Lyly was already neglected when Shakespeare wrote, the highly mannered style which has given the word 'euphuism' to our language superseded by other fashions including that for Sir Philip Sidney's *Arcadia*, eventually published in 1590. Sidney (1554–86) in the pastoral world of the *Arcadia* and his sonnet sequence *Astrophel and Stella* (1591) helped to popularise the Italianate ideals of Castiglione's *The Courtier* (1528), the Platonism of the Florentine academy which attracts Navarre and his book-men, and the Petrarchanism which influences their sonnets. Though Berowne pretends that 'none but minstrels like of sonneting' (IV.3.155), the play coincides with a vogue for the form, and for love-poetry in general. His rejection of the conventional 'Taffeta phrases' and 'three pil'd hyperboles' (V.2.406–7) is itself part of the convention. Even his location of the 'true Promethean fire' in women's eyes that 'show, contain, and nourish all the world' (IV.3.349) would be familiar at a court presided over by a woman, which still remembered Sidney as embodying the Renaissance ideal of soldier, scholar, poet.

Inevitably there were factions and favourites in the course of Elizabeth's long reign, and it has been argued convincingly that some topical rivalry lies behind Shakespeare's play. In 1592 Sir Walter Raleigh (*c*.1552–1618) fell from power and was imprisoned in the Tower, largely because of a secret (and in the Queen's eyes unsuitable) marriage with one of her ladies. Among those pleased to see his discomfiture were the Earl of Essex and his friend the Earl of Southampton, Shakespeare's patron. A play ridiculing the scholarly pretensions of Raleigh and his followers, who included George Chapman (1554–1634), already a poetic rival, might attract both poet and patron. Other controversies of the day, including a long-standing feud between the scholar Gabriel Harvey (*c*.1545–1630) and the pamphleteer Thomas Nashe (*c*.1567–

1601), may have suggested other elements, but the details must remain in doubt.

Though medieval certainties still underpinned Elizabethan society, there was a great outburst of energy bringing changes in politics, in religion, and in the sciences. In *Love's Labour's Lost* the conflicts and developments within the language itself are given exuberant expression. Even in his early plays Shakespeare shows himself able to use the drama as a medium for exploration and discovery. 'Let us once lose our oaths to find ourselves', argues Berowne (IV.3.357), reflecting his creator's own interest in the difference between the roles men adopt, and that secret self which is revealed only in the course of our actions.

A note on the text

Elizabethan playwrights wrote for the stage rather than the page, and publication was by no means the rule. Most of Shakespeare's plays appeared in print only after his death, when in 1623 his fellow actors, John Heminges and Henry Condell, collected them. For their edition, the First Folio, they drew on those plays already published in the quartos (the size of paper supplies the name by which the editions are known) and on the prompt books and manuscripts probably left with the theatre company to which they and Shakespeare belonged. *Love's Labour's Lost* is one of the sixteen plays for which a Quarto survives, dated 1598, and described on the title-page as 'newly corrected and augmented by W. Shakespeare'. This suggests a still earlier version, now lost if ever printed, and there is ample evidence of revision in the Quarto, notably in Berowne's long speech in Act IV Scene 3 with its repetitions, and in the confusion between Rosaline and Katharine in Act II Scene 1. It is generally agreed that the play was conceived and acted early in Shakespeare's career, perhaps in 1594, but rewritten late in 1597 for a special performance at court, in the words of the title-page 'as it was presented before her Highness this last Christmas'. This would mean that the play is a little earlier than *Romeo and Juliet* or *A Midsummer Night's Dream* but not, as was once thought, Shakespeare's first play.

The Folio of 1623 makes some minor corrections to the Quarto text, adds an extra line and as usual divides the play into acts, but there is no evidence that the printer had access to manuscripts unavailable in 1598, so except for obvious misprints modern editors generally follow the Quarto. In these notes, the edition used throughout is the New Arden, edited by Richard David, Methuen, London, 1956.

Full details of critical works mentioned may be found in Part 5, Suggestions for further reading.

Part 2

Summaries
of LOVE'S LABOUR'S LOST

A general summary

Ferdinand, King of Navarre, and three young noblemen take an oath to withdraw from the world and the company of women to devote themselves to study. One of the three, Berowne, is sceptical and his doubts soon prove well-founded. The Princess of France and her three ladies-in-waiting arrive to discuss a disputed loan made by the father of the present King of Navarre to her father, the King of France. In spite of their oaths, the four men fall in love, each composing a sonnet to the lady of his choice. Their attempts at secrecy are defeated, as each is found out in a series of overheard soliloquies. Berowne is the last to be discovered, when his letter falls into the wrong hands. He justifies their backsliding by arguing that women are the one real source of enlightenment, and they resolve to woo their ladies.

The King's subjects experience similar difficulties in avoiding the opposite sex. Costard, a simple countryman, is caught with Jaquenetta, and he has a rival in the person of Armado, a fantastical Spaniard visiting the court. It is Armado's love letter to Jaquenetta, delivered in place of Berowne's to the Princess's lady, Rosaline, that initiates the series of revelations.

The French ladies are not disposed to take the men's change of heart seriously, and when an attendant lord, Boyet, brings news that they are coming to entertain them, disguised as Muscovites, they take advantage of the situation to tease them unmercifully. Since the ladies are masked, the men are persuaded to declare their love to the wrong women, and so stand accused of breaking their oaths twice over.

Armado is asked to arrange further entertainment, and enlists the aid of Holofernes, a pedantic schoolmaster, and Nathaniel the curate. With the help of Costard and the page Moth, and much doubling of the parts, they present a pageant of the Nine Worthies. Rivalries among the players, when Costard reveals that Jaquenetta is pregnant by Armado, and the mockery of the lords, still smarting from their own discomfort at the hands of the ladies, threaten to disrupt the proceedings, when news arrives that the Princess's father is dead.

The men renew their protestations of love, but are told that first they must prove themselves by a year's abstinence from pleasure, and Rosaline insists that Berowne exercise his too-ready wit in a hospital, trying to make sick people laugh. The play ends with the song of the owl and the cuckoo, performed by Holofernes and Nathaniel.

Detailed summaries

Act I Scene 1

The King and three of his nobles have decided to forsake the pleasures of the world for the more lasting rewards of study and contemplation. Two of them, Longaville and Dumain, retain their enthusiasm, but the third, Berowne, has doubts about the value and success of the scheme. Since they are already expecting the arrival of the Princess of France on affairs of state, it will certainly be difficult to escape female company. Nevertheless, Berowne will stand by his word, and the King consoles them with the promise of entertainment from Armado, a Spanish traveller resident at the court, and Costard, a rustic clown.

Costard is now led in by constable Dull, under arrest for being caught with Jaquenetta, a country wench, in spite of the proclamation against converse with the opposite sex. His offence is spelt out in a letter from Armado, written in a ludicrously high-flown style. The King passes sentence: for a week nothing but bran and water with Armado to supervise the punishment. Berowne takes him out, more sceptical than before of the oath they have sworn.

NOTES AND GLOSSARY:
Although Berowne agrees to join the others, his arguments reveal the reasons for their eventual failure. There is something perverse in deciding to 'war against your own affections' (line 9) as the King proposes, and the truths that count are not likely to be discovered by turning your back on life. The arrival of the French princess underlines the practical difficulties, as does Costard's defence of his behaviour with Jaquenetta: 'Such is the simplicity of man to hearken after the flesh' (line 215). The bizarre pedantry of Armado's letter offers another warning to those who prefer book-learning to ordinary living.

scythe's:	Time was traditionally shown as a figure carrying a scythe. By cultivating the life of the mind, and so winning fame, the King hopes to defeat time's stroke and inherit eternity
late edict:	recent proclamation
academe:	academy. Philosophical debating societies of the kind Navarre proposes were fashionable at Renaissance courts, modelled on the original academy of the Greek philosopher Plato (*c*.428–348BC)

cormorant: ravenous

bate: blunt

living art: possibly a translation of the Latin *ars vivendi*, the moral philosophy which the Romans inherited from the Stoic philosophers of the third century BC who practised the austere self-discipline advocated here by Navarre

That his own hand may strike his honour down: that his signature may expose him to the disgrace of breaking his promise

branch: detail of the conditions

Fat paunches have lean wits: gluttony diminishes mental powers

mortified: dead to the promptings of the flesh

all these: his three companions

liege: lord

wink: close one's eyes

wont: accustomed

By yea and nay: without exaggerated oaths

barr'd: shut out

common sense: ordinary uninformed intelligence

and not break my troth: without breaking my word

train: entice

falsely: treacherously

Light seeking light doth light of light beguile: the eyes seeking truth are dimmed by too much reading

a fairer eye: the eye of a fair lady, whose beauty dazzles but inspires the lover more effectively than any book. This idea, a commonplace among the poets of Shakespeare's youth writing under the influence of the Italian sonneteer Petrarch (1304–74), is developed and modified in the course of the play

heed: either the object or the subject of attention

saucy: impertinent

plodders: scholars who depend on laborious accumulation of detail rather than real insight

godfathers: sponsors at a baptism, after whom the child was often named

those that walk and wot not what they are: ordinary men, ignorant of the names of the stars, may admire them more than pedantic astronomers

fame: here, in perhaps deliberate contrast with the opening line, empty reputation

green geese: young geese, bred to be ready for the goose fairs held in May. Berowne is hinting that his young friends may soon find themselves victims

rhyme:	when spelt 'rime' meaning hoar-frost, so prompting the reply in the next line
sneaping:	nipping
Before the birds have any cause to sing:	Berowne thinks his friends premature in preening themselves on their own wisdom
May's new-fangled shows:	the gaudy blossoms of the spring
like of:	like
to study now it is too late:	they should learn from experience rather than try to go back to school
Climb o'er the house to unlock the little gate:	make a labour of something easy and natural
barbarism:	ignorance, lack of culture
Marry:	a corruption of 'By the Virgin Mary'
gentility:	good manners
is overshot:	misses its aim
so won, so lost:	if a town can only be captured by burning it to the ground, it is of no value to the victors
of force:	necessarily
lie:	stay
affects:	passions
grace:	favours stemming from God
in attainder of:	condemned to
suggestions:	temptations
quick:	lively
mint:	manufactory
complements:	accomplishments
mutiny:	strife
hight:	is named, already archaic in Shakespeare's time
tawny:	olive skinned
debate:	conflict
minstrelsy:	entertainment usually provided by musicians
wight:	man, again appropriately archaic
fire-new:	brand new
swain:	rustic, countryman
reprehend:	represent, Dull intends to say, the first of many such mistakes
farborough:	thirdborough or constable
Signior:	form of address for gentleman
contempts:	he means contents
magnificent Armado:	the expression would remind the audience of the Spanish Armada sent against England in 1588, especially if the commentators are right in seeing Armado as in part a satirical portrait of Sir Walter Raleigh, celebrated for his naval exploits

A high hope for a low heaven: heaven is the reward for hope in God, but Armado's words would be a poor recompense for such hope

forbear: refrain from

style: punning on 'stile'

The matter: the substance

taken with the manner: punning on the legal term 'mainour', the whole phrase meaning 'caught in the act'

In manner and form following: another legal formula, and Costard puns on manner/manor and form meaning 'bench'

correction: punishment

simplicity: foolishness. The Quarto prints 'sinplicitie' which may be still another pun

the welkin's vicegerent: heaven's deputy

dominator: ruler

but so: worth little

besieged: afflicted

sable-coloured: black

humour: moods were supposed to have a physiological origin, melancholy originating in the black bile, one of the four fluids which governed the human body

commend: entrust

The time when?: the mechanical formulas of Armado's letter parody the rhetorical exercises in the school-books of Shakespeare's youth

ycleped: another antique form of 'called'

preposterous: highly improper

snow-white pen: made from a goose-quill

curious knotted: in Elizabethan gardens the flower beds were laid out in elaborate patterns

base minnow: poor fish

unlettered: illiterate

vassal: inferior

sorted: associated

continent canon: law enforcing chastity

passion: grieve

pricks: urges

meed: reward

carriage: behaviour

weaker vessel: women were traditionally regarded as the weaker sex, their honour more fragile

vessel: recipient

the best for the worst: the best in being so bad

sirrah:	my man, a form of address for social inferiors
so varied too:	the proclamation has covered all varieties of women
serve my turn:	satisfy me, not as an excuse (the king's meaning) but as an answer to Costard's sexual desire
lay:	bet

prosperity! Affliction: Costard mixes up the two words

Act I Scene 2

Armado enters, in low spirits, with his page Moth, and in answer to his teasing confesses he is in love with Jaquenetta. He searches for precedents for a love so out of keeping with his character as a soldier and a gentleman. Dull comes in to hand over Costard, and to take Jaquenetta to the park as a dairymaid, where Armado promises to visit her. Left alone, he meditates on his love and resolves to commit it to paper.

NOTES AND GLOSSARY:
The humour of the opening exchange depends partly on the physical contrast between the gaunt Armado and the diminutive Moth, the 'tough signior' and the 'tender juvenal' (lines 11-12). Ironically, Armado who arrested Costard in the previous scene for his attentions to Jaquenetta, now finds himself infatuated with the same girl. Love proves too strong for the old soldier: 'Cupid's butt-shaft is too hard for Hercules' club' (lines 165-6).

imp:	child
juvenal:	juvenile, but with a pun on the Roman satirist Juvenal (*c*.60–130 AD). This has led commentators to identify Moth with Thomas Nashe (*c*.1567–1601), a pamphleteer elsewhere referred to as 'young Juvenal, that biting satirist'
Signor:	with a pun on 'senior'
congruent epitheton:	suitable epithet
appertinent:	appropriate
condign:	well deserved
thou heat'st my blood:	you make me angry
crossed:	opposed
crosses:	coins, often stamped with a cross. Moth is mocking Armado's poverty
thrice told:	multiplied by three
ill:	poor
tapster:	one who served drinks at an inn
gamester:	card or dice player
the gross sum of deuce-ace:	the addition of two and one

vulgar:	common people
dancing horse:	in Shakespeare's time, Morocco, a performing horse, was famous for such tricks
fine figure:	ingenious comparison
cipher:	a nothing
reprobate:	depraved
courtesy:	a bow or compliment. The French were renowned (and despised) for their proficiency in such arts
outswear:	forswear, renounce
Hercules:	the Greek hero is best remembered for his feats of strength in carrying out the twelve labours imposed on him by King Eurystheus, though in some versions of the myth he undertook the labours for love of the king's daughter
carriage:	bearing. One of the biblical strong man Samson's exploits was the removal of the gates of the city of Gaza. The story of this and of his fortunes in love is told in the Book of Judges, Chapter 16
well-knit:	strongly made
complexion:	colouring or humour. Moth understands it in the second sense
all the four:	the four humours, blood, phlegm, yellow and black bile, which governed character
sea-water green:	not one of the humours, but a colour associated with youth and love
a green wit:	a lively intelligence. Delilah, Samson's love, was clever enough to betray him to his enemies by revealing the source of his strength
immaculate:	spotless
invocation:	Moth calls on, or invokes, the qualities inherited from his parents
Which native she doth owe:	which she possesses naturally. Her colouring, Moth's rhyme suggests, is an untrustworthy guide to her character
the King and the Beggar:	Armado sees a parallel between his own case and the story of King Cophetua who scorned love but then fell for a beggar-maid. An alternative title for the ballad, *Cupid's Revenge*, points the moral
digression:	transgression
rational hind:	intelligent rustic
light:	unchaste
suffer:	allow
penance:	pleasance, or pleasure, he means
day-woman:	dairymaid

on a full stomach:	when well fed, but with a secondary meaning of 'courageously'
fast and loose:	cheating, an expression derived from a game played by gypsies
desolation:	the opposite of what the sense requires, as in Costard's last words in Act I Scene 1
as little patience:	again, he must mean 'as much'
base . . . baser . . . basest:	another of the mechanical constructions favoured by Armado and mocked by Shakespeare
argument:	proof
familiar:	attendant spirit, usually evil
Solomon:	Biblical king famous for his wisdom, but in old age 'his wives turned away his heart after other gods' (1 Kings 11:4)
Cupid's butt-shaft:	Cupid was the mischievous god of love whose arrows pierced the heart of those destined to feel the passion. A butt-shaft was an arrow without barbs, yet it could overcome the club which Hercules generally carried
too much odds:	has too great an advantage over
the first and second cause:	part of the elaborate etiquette governing the 'duello', or practice of duelling
passado:	forward thrust with the sword
boy:	Cupid was eternally young
turn sonnet:	compose a sonnet

Act II Scene 1

The Princess of France enters with her ladies-in-waiting and sends Boyet to notify Navarre of her arrival. In his absence they discuss the men who have vowed themselves to study. Each lady seems to have a special interest in one of the three. Boyet returns with news that the King will not admit them, but is coming himself to meet them in the park. Understandably irritated, they greet the King and his nobles and move on to discuss the matter which has brought the princess here. The father of the present king had lent two hundred thousand crowns to the King of France, on the surety of part of Aquitaine. The French king now claims to have repaid half the original debt and wants another two hundred thousand crowns, part of which he thinks can be covered by ceding Aquitaine to Navarre. Navarre knows nothing of any repayment, and although willing to write off part of the existing debt in deference to the Princess, finds her father's terms too unreasonable to meet. The Princess claims to have documents proving the repayment but 'the packet is not come' (line 163) and we hear no more of it in the course of the play. With many apologies Navarre withdraws, promising to visit them again next day. The nobles stay behind to press Boyet for information about the three ladies, and when they leave Boyet tells the princess that he thinks the King too has not escaped heart-whole.

NOTES AND GLOSSARY:

The Princess's rebuke to the flattering Boyet and the 'painted flourish' (line 14) of his praise expresses an awareness running through the whole play of the distinction between reality and the language which can conceal or distort it. If the ladies have a criticism of the three young lords, it is that they see everything as an opportunity to exercise their wit without stopping to think of their power to wound. So they are on their guard to resist the opening advances of the men. Ironically, Boyet's speech on 'the heart's still rhetoric' (line 227) is one of the most verbose and artificial in the play.

summon up your dearest spirits: collect all your wits

embassy: ambassador

prodigal of all dear grace: lavish with your charms. Boyet rightly thinks her beauty may accomplish more than any legal claims

mean: nothing special

flourish: ornamentation

chapmen: merchants or peddlars, with a possible pun on the name of George Chapman, a rival poet and dramatist and a member of the coterie led by Sir Walter Raleigh probably satirised in this play

task the tasker: Boyet has been instructing the Princess how to proceed; now she instructs him to approach the King

fame: rumour, report

best-moving fair solicitor: most persuasive advocate

humble-visag'd: meek-faced

sovereign parts: unrivalled accomplishments

would well: wishes kindly

soil: blemish

gloss: bright appearance

blunt: rough, unfeeling

Such short-liv'd wits do wither as they grow: this kind of quickness does not ripen into wisdom

least knowing ill: without intending any harm

shape: appearance

withal: with

conceit's expositor: expressing his thought

play truant: leave their affairs to listen

competitors:	partners
address'd:	ready
unpeopled:	without the servants necessary to entertain guests
the roof of this court:	the sky
too base to be mine:	she deserves something better than accommodation out of doors
will shall break it will:	Navarre's oath seems mere wilfulness to the Princess, so she sees no reason why he should not make an exception for them
his ignorance were wise:	he would be wiser to know nothing of such an undertaking
house-keeping:	hospitality
vouchsafe:	agree
suddenly:	immediately
suit:	request
Brabant:	part of the Netherlands
long for you:	because of you
fair befall your mask:	good luck go with you. Since the ladies are apparantly masked, as again in Act V Scene 2, Berowne does not know to whom he is speaking. In the Quarto edition the conversation involves Katharine, but in the Folio edition Rosaline is the masked lady. Shakespeare may have intended a case of mistaken identity, but then decided to keep the idea for the later scene, with some confusion in the text as a result
intimate:	tell of
disbursed:	paid out
as neither have:	though in fact neither of us has
not demands:	does not demand. The French king will give up Aquitaine rather than pay the hundred thousand crowns
gelded:	curtailed, reduced in value
unseeming:	seeming not to
arrest your word:	hold you to your promise
acquittances:	receipts
specialities:	special contracts or sealed documents
liberal reason:	reasonable argument
make tender of:	offer
deem:	think
consort:	accompany
fool:	term of affection rather than contempt
let it blood:	bleeding was a cure for many ailments, used by the 'physic' or medicine of the time

no point: not at all; with a pun on the next phrase

Katherine her name: the Quarto this time prints 'Rosaline' but it seems reasonable that each of the men should single out 'his' lady

an: if

light: with the familiar pun on 'unchaste'

your beard: allusions to beards seem often to have figured in insults

choler: anger

by good hap: as it happens

mad-cap: wild, dare-devil

every jest but a word: Boyet thinks his wit is merely verbal

take him at his word: reply to him in his own fashion

grapple: in naval battles ships would lay hold of each other with iron grapnels before boarding for hand to hand fighting

board: with a pun on 'bourd' or jest

ships: pronounced like 'sheeps' at this period, so an opportunity for further punning

no common, though several: common land was available to all, but enclosed land or 'severals' were private property. Rosaline's two lips are also 'several' in being more than one, hence the pun

jangling: contending, clashing

still rhetoric: silent language, dumb eloquence

infected: love-sick

his behaviours did make their retire: all his faculties retreated to the stronghold of his eye, to peep out at the enemy. Vanquished by the Princess's beauty, Navarre can only stand and stare

thorough: through

agate: semi-precious stone often engraved for rings

his form: the Princess's image impressed on his heart

did make their repair: all the other senses throng to share the eye's vision of the Princess

tend'ring their own worth from where they were glass'd: Navarre's faculties now concentrated and 'glass'd' in his eye, and striving to show themselves off are the Princess's for the asking. Love is as clearly written in his face as comment in the margin of a book

our pavillion: presumably the King has set up a large tent for the ladies' stay

dispos'd: inclined to make fun

made a mouth of his eye: expressed what his eye would speak

love-monger:	match-maker
Venus:	in Classical mythology she was the goddess of love, Cupid's mother and wife of Vulcan, lame blacksmith of the gods. Judging by his looks, Rosaline suggests, if Boyet is Cupid's grandfather, it is on the paternal side
mad:	outrageous
too hard for me:	more than I can manage

Act III Scene 1

Moth entertains Armado's melancholy with a song and gives him some advice, then is sent to fetch Costard who is to carry a love-letter to Jaquenetta. Costard enters rubbing his shin, and his injury is the occasion for a series of jokes and riddles in which all three join. He is then given his freedom, and a small tip, and sent off with the letter. He now meets Berowne who also gives him a letter, to be delivered to Rosaline, and a somewhat larger tip. Left alone, Berowne laments the fact that he who has always mocked lovers should himself be in love, and with a woman whose looks and character suggest that he will be made to suffer for it.

NOTES AND GLOSSARY:
This act artfully draws attention to the parallels between Armado, introduced as a laughing-stock for the young lords, and Berowne, the hero of the play. Both depend on Costard to deliver their letters, and in matters of love the difference between them seems only that between Armado's 'remuneration' (line 128) and Berowne's 'guerdon' (line 165). Berowne's closing soliloquy recalls Armado's words at the end of Act I. The scene with Moth, Costard, Armado and their 'l'envoy' can seem tedious on the page, and there may be allusions in 'the fox, the ape, and the humble-bee' (line 82) now lost to us, but on stage like so much else in this play it can still amuse.

warble:	sing
Concolinel:	either the title or refrain of a song now lost
enlargement:	freedom
festinately:	in a hurry
brawl:	a dance, and also a quarrel. Armado understands it in the second sense
complete:	lacking no accomplishment
canary:	another dance
humour:	indulge
penthouse-like:	tilted forward, like the canopy over a shop

thin-belly doublet: close-fitting jacket, either pinched in to conform with fashion, or because the lover is pining away

snip and away: a snatch, or snippet, then off to something else

complements: courtesies

nice: lascivious

of note: noteworthy, highly regarded

penny: pennyworth. The phrase and later references to 'pierce' or purse reinforce the connection with Thomas Nashe, author of *Pierce Penilesse* (1592)

The hobby-horse is forgot: a man wearing an arrangement round his waist to make him look as if he was riding a horse featured in folk dances then and now. The expression occurs here and in other plays of the period, often with nostalgic overtones, and perhaps comes from an old song. 'Hobby-horse' was also slang for prostitute, as was 'hackney' a few lines later, and Armado takes it in this sense

out of heart: discouraged

sympathised: there is an affinity between the messenger and Armado who sends the message; both are asinine, in Moth's opinion

slow-gaited: slow moving

Minime: (*Latin*) 'by no means'

Sweet smoke of rhetoric: a fine cloud of words, though it is the gun that suggests smoke

Thump: the sound of the cannon

costard: an apple, and by extension a head, so incongruous as the victim of a bruised shin

l'envoy: lines at the close of a work, addressed directly to the reader (see line 79). Armado wants the end of Moth's story

egma: Costard's mishearing of 'enigma' or riddle, which he understands as some cure for his shin

salve: a salute or leave-taking, and so related to the 'l'envoy', but also when pronounced as one syllable, a soothing remedy, like the leaves of the plantain

mail: bag, wallet

spleen: the organ which regulated violent emotions

ridiculous: leading to laughter

inconsiderate: unthinking

tofore been sain: previously been stated

still at odds: always fighting, and constituting an odd number, three

stayed: righted

A good l'envoy, ending in the goose: Moth finds Armado's words apt, because goose meant fool (his opinion of his master) and there may be a pun on *l'oye*, the Old French word for goose

sold him a bargain: made a fool of him

that's flat: that's the truth

sensibly: feelingly

enfranchise: free, but Costard again misunderstands. 'Goose' was also slang for prostitute, hence his pretended alarm at the suggestion

purgation: clearing of an offence, but no doubt with a pun on the medical sense of cleaning the bowels

significant: communication

remuneration: payment

ward: guard or defence

sequel: what follows, so again linked with 'l'envoy'

incony: darling

farthing: coin worth a quarter of a penny

inkle: linen tape

carries it: wins the purchase

French crown: a coin, but punning on the bald scalp caused by syphilis, the 'French disease'

out of: without

knave: lad, fellow

your worship: your honour

villain: like 'knave' when addressed to a character of Costard's class not intended offensively

train: retinue of followers

counsel: communication

guerdon: payment, reward

a'leven-pence farthing better: and so, evidently, a shilling

in print: exactly, to the letter

forsooth: in truth

beadle: officer responsible for punishing minor offences

pedant: schoolmaster

the boy: Cupid

magnificent: proud, and so not easily domineered

wimpled: blindfold. Cupid shot his arrows at random

purblind: completely blind

giant-dwarf: paradoxically linking Cupid's great power and small size

dan: Don, a title

folded arms: the traditional pose of the lover

malcontents: rebellious or discontented persons

plackets:	openings in women's petticoats, and so by extension the women themselves, usually in a bawdy sense
codpieces:	part of male costume covering the genitals, and so by extension the genitals themselves
imperator:	absolute ruler
paritors:	ecclesiastical officers, frequently concerned with sexual offences
field:	battlefield
colours:	distinctive uniform showing allegiance to a particular leader
tumbler's hoop:	the hoops used by acrobats or tumblers often had coloured ribbons attached
Still a-repairing:	always having to be repaired
out of frame:	out of order
whitely:	pale
velvet:	black
the deed:	the act of love
Argus:	in classical mythology, Juno, queen of the gods, set Argus to keep watch over Io, a nymph transformed into a heifer, pursued by her husband Jupiter. In spite of Argus's hundred eyes Jupiter's son Mercury succeeded in outwitting him
eunuch:	castrated men were employed to guard the women in the harems of the East
watch:	lose sleep
Go to:	come now, surely not
my lady . . . Joan:	opposite ends of the female spectrum

Act IV Scene 1

The Princess and her ladies-in-waiting are hunting, attended by one of the King's foresters, when Costard arrives with a letter for Rosaline. By mistake he delivers Armado's letter, intended for Jaquenetta, but the ladies break the seal and read it. The Princess goes out, and Boyet teases Rosaline about her admirer Berowne, but in a battle of wits full of *double-entendres* she and the ladies get the better of him, leaving Costard to reflect on the 'sweet jests' (line 143) to which love gives rise in all its manifestations.

NOTES AND GLOSSARY:
The Princess's pretended misunderstanding of the forester recalls her clash with Boyet at the opening of Act II. Language, especially when addressed to women, seems full of pitfalls. Armado's letter is in a style

already outmoded when Shakespeare wrote, though fashionable in its day and associated above all with the first English novel, *Euphues*, by John Lyly. Lyly was also the leading playwright of the 1580s and an influence on Shakespeare's own comedies. Hunting and archery were popular pastimes and a favourite source of puns and metaphors in the game of love, as we see in the exchanges between Boyet and the ladies.

a'was: he was
mounting: ambitious, with a pun on horseriding
despatch: dismissal
play the murderer: shoot the deer, driven past the place where the huntsmen were stationed
coppice: small wood
the fairest shoot: the best shot, but she punningly takes him to mean the most beautiful
alack for woe: I am sorry indeed
never paint me now: it is too late to flatter me
mend the brow: improve a face without beauty
good my glass: my good mirror, ironically to the forester for accurately reflecting her appearance
more than due: more than they deserve
inherit: possess
by merit: by merit of her action in tipping him. She pretends that it is not her innate worth which receives praise, but her 'giving hand', and makes a parallel with the distinction in religion between 'justification by faith' and the 'heresy' of 'justification by works', one of the main points of difference between Protestants and Catholics
shooting well is then accounted ill: there is a conflict between the desire to shoot well and pity for the wounded animal
Thus will I save my credit: by shooting well she hopes to show that praise is deserved
Not wounding, pity would not let me do't: if she misses she will say it was out of pity for the deer
If wounding: if she wounds without killing it is because she is thirsty for praise rather than blood
out of question: certainly
Glory grows guilty of detested crimes: some editors see this speech as an allusion to the crime of the Protestant Henry of Navarre who in 1593 became a convert to Catholicism to secure the French throne. This may explain what seems over-fastidiousness if hunting is all that is involved

Glory: the desire for glory

an outward part: a relatively superficial gain when set against the promptings of the heart

curst: shrewish

that self-sovereignty: that same control of their softer feelings. Boyet is ironical; he believes there is no such conflict in shrewish wives, who lord it over their husbands because it is their nature to do so

Only for praise: the Princess persists in thinking well of her sex

the commonwealth: perhaps the select company bound by the King's oath, but probably simply 'one of the people'

God dig-you-den: God give you good evening

the greatest lady, the highest: Costard is thinking of social status, but the Princess understands him literally

as slender as my wit: as small as my intelligence

What's your will: what is it you want? The Princess is offended to be thought fatter than her ladies

capon: chicken, but also a love-letter, from the French word *poulet*. To 'carve', then, is to open the letter

importeth: concerns

break the neck of the wax: the sealing-wax has no neck, though the 'chicken' would

have commiseration: take pity. Throughout the letter elaborate phrases cover commonplace thoughts

vassal: servant

illustrate: illustrious

indubitate: unmistakable

Zenelophon: elsewhere Penelophon, the beggar-maid whom Cophetua was driven to love

'veni, vidi, vici': (*Latin*) 'I came, I saw, I overcame', a phrase in a letter by Julius Caesar (*c*.102–44BC), the Roman emperor, famous for his military exploits

annothanize: annotate or anatomise

vulgar: common tongue, here plain English

'videlicet': (*Latin*) 'namely'

catastrophe: conclusion of a play, not necessarily disastrous as in the modern sense

nuptial: marriage

lowliness: low social position

tittles: small, and so worthless, particles

profane my lips: lower myself to kiss

dearest design of industry: sincerest intentions of service

the Nemean lion: in Greek legend the first of the labours of Hercules was to kill a monstrous lion

repasture:	food. Armado is warning Jaquenetta to submit or become 'food for his rage'
indited:	composed
vane:	weathercock, something self-important and unstable
going o'er it erewhile:	reading over the letter just now, with a pun on 'stile'
keeps:	stays
phantasime:	fantastic
Monarcho:	an Italian who imagined himself monarch of the world, well known in London in the 1570s
Here, sweet:	addressed to Rosaline, who will have better luck another day
suitor:	with a pun on 'shooter', both words being similar in pronunciation
continent:	that which contains
Finely put off:	well managed!
horns:	and the deer that wear them, but horns were also the mark of the cuckold, and Boyet suggests that if Rosaline marries she will deceive her husband within the year
deer:	with a very familiar pun on 'dear'
If we choose by the horns:	if the target is a man easily cuckolded
wrangle:	wrestle
at the brow:	where the cuckolds horns would grow
hit lower:	perhaps through the heart, with Cupid's arrow, but probably lower still. The rest of the scene though about archery is full of allusions depending on the fact that to 'hit it' meant to 'score' sexually, to have sexual intercourse
that was a man:	that was old
King Pepin:	died 768
Guinever:	wife of Arthur, early and largely mythical King of Britain
the hit it:	name of a dance tune
troth:	faith
fit it:	match their words to the tune and occasion
mark:	target, punning on to 'mark' or notice. Like 'prick', indicating the centre of the target by a stripped twig or 'pin' inserted in it, the term has an obvious bawdy sense
mete:	aim
your hand is out:	out of practice, off-form. Boyet takes up the idea literally, with further indecent hints

Wide o'the bow-hand: wide of the mark, and so missing the target
clout: pin marking centre of target
get the upshoot: the upshot, or upper hand, also cause ejaculation
greasily: bawdily
pricks: archery, but with the continuing sexual allusion
rubbing: a technical term from the game of bowls, as one bowl rubs against another and so has difficulty in reaching the target
owl: a wise person, at least in appearance. At that date there would be a full rhyme with 'bowl'
so obscenely: an accurate description of the previous conversation, though the sense seems to require something more commendatory
Armado to th'one side: Armado on the one hand. Costard's abrupt reversion to Armado has been seen as a reference to some lost appearance by the Spaniard and his page in this scene, but he may just be savouring the absurd picture conjured up by Armado's letter
a most pathetical nit: a most endearing little creature
Sola, sola: a hunting call

Act IV Scene 2

Two more of Navarre's subjects enter, Holofernes the schoolmaster and Nathaniel the curate, discussing the hunting. Constable Dull is with them, though he can understand very little of their learned conversation. Holofernes improvises a rhyming epitaph on the deer the Princess has killed, and Nathaniel is suitably impressed. The illiterate Jaquenetta and Costard come to ask them to read the letter she has received, supposedly from Armado but in fact from Berowne as a result of Costard's earlier mistake. It takes the form of a sonnet in praise of Rosaline, and in view of the proclamation, Holofernes sends Jaquenetta to the King with the letter. He then leaves to dine with the father of one of his pupils, inviting Nathaniel and Dull to accompany him.

NOTES AND GLOSSARY:
Although the King does not offer Holofernes as another source of entertainment for his young friends, his pedantry is as ridiculous as Armado's excesses. His self-importance, based on little more than scraps of Latin remembered from the school-room, suggests that paper and ink are not an adequate diet for the intellect. Even Dull has a firmer grasp of actualities; at least he knows the deer was a pricket. Berowne's sonnet forms part of the running argument between book-learning and love as the source of real understanding.

reverend: respectable

in the testimony of: with the blessing of

sanguis, in blood: luckily Holofernes translates his Latin as he goes along. 'In blood' means in prime condition

pomewater: apple popular at the time

anon: soon

crab: crab-apple

the epithets are sweetly varied: Holofernes habitually offers several alternatives for ordinary words to fill out his sentences

a buck of the first head: a full-grown male deer. The head of horns indicates the age of the animal

'haud credo': (*Latin*) I think not. Dull apparently hears this as 'old grey doe', and a doe being a female deer, protests that it was a pricket, a two-year-old buck

barbarous intimation: ignorant remark

'facere': (*Latin*) to make

replication: repetition

undressed: plain

uncomfirmed: unauthorised

twice-sod: twice boiled, the Latin *bis coctus*, meaning double-dyed or immovable

dainties: sweet things, delicacies

Which we: that we

So were there a patch set on learning: it would be to set a fool to study

'omne bene': (*Latin*) all is for the best

an old father: some learned scholastic authority or father of the church

brook: endure. Nathaniel's aphorism seems to suggest that Dull's insensitivity at least makes him serviceable

Cain: Adam's eldest son, as recorded in the Bible in the Book of Genesis

Dictynna: in classical mythology Diana, goddess of the moon, also known as Phoebe and Luna

raught: reached

The allusion holds in the exchange: if we replace Dictynna with Adam, the implication still applies

collusion: Dull misunderstands

pollution: wrong again

extemperol: improvised on the spot

'perge': (*Latin*) proceed

abrogate scurrility: avoid indecency

affect the letter: practise alliteration, as further evidence of his skill

preyful: predatory or killing much prey

sore:
: a four-year-old buck, but punning on 'sore' as something painful

put 'ell to sore:
: the 'ell' borrowed from 'yell' makes 'sorel', a buck in its third year. 'Ell' or L is also the Latin numeral for fifty, hence the fifty sores two lines later, and the hundred when yet another L is added

or else sore'll:
: the playfulness seems merely verbal here unless the spelling should be 'sorell' as in the Quarto, in which case the line may mean 'the people begin to hoot either a wounded pricket or a sorel'

talent:
: gift or accomplishment, but punning on a bird's claw or 'talon'. 'Claw' also means to flatter, as does Nathaniel

ventricle:
: a division of the brain

pia mater:
: membrane covering the brain, and hence the brain itself

Mehercle:
: By Hercules!

want:
: lack

capable:
: with a secondary meaning of old enough to marry

put it to them:
: make them work, but with a secondary sexual sense, like 'capable' and 'under you' a few lines earlier. Feeling he has said too much about his extra-academic activities, he breaks off with a Latin tag

'vir sapit qui pauca loquitur':
: (*Latin*) with few words a wise man will say much

a soul feminine:
: a woman

Person:
: parson, addressed to Nathaniel the curate

'quasi':
: (*Latin*) as if

hogshead:
: large wine-barrel, to be broached or 'pierced'. Costard takes up the pun on 'pierce-one'

a good lustre of conceit: a gleam of wit

turf of earth:
: a clod, or simple person

pearl enough for a swine: alluding to the biblical proverb of 'casting pearls before swine' or offering advice to those incapable of profitting by it. Holofernes is surprised to find so much wit in the unlettered Costard

'Facile precor':
: a hackneyed quotation from the fifteenth-century Latin author Battista Spagnuoli, surnamed Mantuan. Either Holofernes or the printer gets the first word wrong: it should be 'Fauste', and the whole phrase 'O Faustus, I pray you while all our cattle are chewing in the cool shade'

staff:
: stanza or group of lines

'Chi non ti vede, non ti pretia': (*Italian*) only those who do not see you do not praise you

Ut, re, sol: do,re,me, the tonic sol-fa which Holofernes would be expected to teach, though he seems to confuse the order of the notes

Horace: a Latin poet (65-8BC), known especially as author of the *Odes*, which have been widely read in British schools and universities

'lege, domine': (*Latin*) read, master

osiers: willows. Under Rosaline's influence Berowne's determination, unshakable as the oak tree, has yielded like the flexible willow

bias: tendency

comprehend: encompass

wonder: admiration

Which is to me some praise: since she combines all the virtues ('parts'), it is some credit to him that he admires her

Jove: chief of the gods, commanding thunder and lightning

Celestial: heavenly

apostrophus: punctuation indicating an omitted syllable

supervise: look over

canzonet: short song or lyric

numbers ratified: verses metrically correct but with no spark of poetry

'caret': (*Latin*) it is missing

Ovidius Naso: Ovid (43BC-AD17) is the Roman poet best remembered as author of the *Metamorphoses*, one of the most influential books for the poets of Shakespeare's generation. 'Naso' is also Latin for 'with the nose', hence Holofernes's pun on smelling

odoriferous: sweet-smelling

jerks: sudden flashes of wit

'Imitari': (*Latin*) imitate

tired: attired or harnessed

damosella: damsel or virgin

strange: foreign, though Berowne is not one of the Princess's party

superscript: what is written at the top of the letter

intellect: intelligence, meaning

votaries: those who have taken a vow

framed: composed

sequent: follower

by the way of progression: in its progress

Trip and go: name of a dance, here meaning 'step lightly'

Stay not thy compliment: don't delay to curtsey on leaving (her 'd

Have with thee: off you go

very religiously: very properly, in upholding the King's orde
strictly

colourable colours: plausible pretexts or excuses

for the pen: for the writing, but not for the contents

before repast: before the meal, when if Nathaniel will say
customary prayer or 'grace' Holofernes will
that he is welcome, or in Italian 'ben venuto'

saith the text: we do not know what authority Nathaniel has
mind, but the idea is a commonplace

certes: certainly

'pauca verba': (*Latin*) few words, cutting short Dull's expected
protestations, though he has in fact said nothing

the gentles: the nobility

their game: hunting

recreation: refreshment

Act IV Scene 3

Berowne enters with a paper, presumably another sonnet for Rosaline,
but hides when the King approaches. He too has a love poem, for the
Princess, which he reads and then leaves where he hopes she will find it.
He steps aside as Longaville comes in, with a sonnet expressing his love
for Maria. In his turn Longaville takes cover at the arrival of Dumain,
but when he has heard him read his poem, inspired by Katharine,
comes forward to reproach him. The King then emerges to chide
Longaville for his hypocrisy. Finally Berowne climbs down from the
tree where he has been hiding to expose the King and to reprove all
three for breaking their oaths. But he breaks off when he sees Jaquenetta and Costard bringing a letter, a letter which, in spite of his efforts
to destroy it, is revealed as his own sonnet to Rosaline. After some
wrangling about the respective merits of their four ladies, realising that
they are all in the same dilemma the others ask Berowne to undertake
their defence. He does so in a long speech arguing that since women
hold the key to all real knowledge, only by abandoning their oaths can
they be true to their original aim. They set about wooing the Princess
and her ladies without more delay.

NOTES AND GLOSSARY:
That the four lovers should write sonnets, though not all of the regular
fourteen-line form, reflects the prevailing fashion of the early 1590s.
Although the poems implicitly recognise the foolishness of the young

men's earlier ambition to war against 'the huge army of the world's desires' (I.1.10), their highly artificial rhetoric is another form of self-deception. This scene marks a turning-point for them, but they still have to convince the ladies, and Berowne forsees trouble.

coursing:	chasing
pitched a toil:	set a snare
toiling in a pitch:	struggling but unable to escape, with perhaps a recollection of Rosaline's eyes as 'two pitch-balls' (III.1.192)
set:	sit
as mad as Ajax:	in Greek legend the hero Ajax, driven mad by the goddess Athene, slaughtered a herd of cattle imagining that he was revenging himself on his fellow Greeks
well proved again o' my side:	Berowne's arguments demonstrate that he is a fool and in love
lie in my throat:	tell a real falsehood, not a merely verbal one
were in:	were in the same predicament
God gave him grace to groan:	May he prove to be as lovesick as myself
bird-bolt:	blunt arrow, suitable for a boy like Cupid
left pap:	left breast, covering the heart
eye-beams:	glances
The night of dew:	tears
as a coach:	each teardrop carries her reflection, like a coach
shade folly:	hide foolishness
like a perjure, wearing papers:	criminals were sometimes forced to wear labels, or papers, indicating their crime
two that I know:	the King and Berowne himself
triumviry:	group of three rulers
corner-cap:	three-cornered cap worn by judges
Tyburn:	where the gallows stood, triangular in shape. Love is seen as a tyrannical power, executing those foolish enough to oppose it
stubborn:	difficult to shape
numbers:	verses
guards:	embroideries
hose:	close-fitting tights, worn by men in the days before trousers
shop:	codpiece. Without the decorative camouflage of verse, lust ('wanton Cupid') will be revealed in all its coarse actuality
Exhals't this vapour-vow:	the sun draws up vapours to itself, just as the lady draws out his vow, so absolving him from it

the liver vein: the liver was thought to be the seat of passion, and Longaville's verses show the effects

out o' th'way: having gone astray

Company: someone is coming

all hid, an old infant play: from Berowne's superior viewpoint, the lovers seem involved in a children's game

o'er-eye: observe

More sacks to the mill: more work to do

woodcocks: game-birds, proverbially foolish

coxcomb: fool, from the 'cock's-comb' cap worn by the court jester

corporal: military officer, four to a regiment. Berowne sees himself and the others as forced to enlist under love's colours. There is also a pun on 'corporeal'; the 'divine Kate' is only flesh and blood

for foul have amber quoted: her amber coloured hair makes amber itself seem dull in comparison

raven: a bird or 'fowl', though black in colour

Her shoulder is with child: she is round shouldered and stooping. Blinded by his love for Rosaline, Berowne can see no attraction in Dumain's Katharine

a good word: Amen, the conventional ending of a prayer

incision: cuts for bleeding

saucers: cupping-dishes used to catch the blood

misprision: misunderstanding

ode: poem of no particular form at this date

passing fair: exceptionally beautiful

unmeet: unsuitable

Ethiop: dark as an Ethiopian, rather than the fashionable fair-haired beauty. In Greek mythology Juno was the wife of Jove, renowned for her beauty

deny himself for Jove: renounce his divinity

fasting: hungry

Ill, to example ill: wrong-doing, by teaching others to do wrong, would make his own fault less culpable

dote: love excessively

thy love is far from charity: it is no charitable impulse which leads Dumain to want to share his situation with others

taken napping: caught out, taken unawares

his wreathed arms athwart: arms folded across the chest, the lover's posture

shrouded: hidden

reek: come from you like smoke

worms: an expression of pity rather than contempt

no coaches: referring to the King's sonnet (line 33)

Tush: nonsense

none but minstrels like of sonneting: only entertainers could enjoy writing love-poetry

o'ershot: in the wrong, out of the true path

mote: speck of dust. See the Bible, Matthew 8:5: 'Thou hypocrite, first cast out the beam out of thine own eye; and then shalt thou see clearly to cast out the mote out of thy brother's eye'

teen: grief

gnat: small insignificant creature

whipping a gig: reduced to whipping a top, like a child

tune a jig: play or sing a dance tune, quite inappropriate to Solomon's gravity and wisdom

Nestor: in Greek legend, one of the oldest and wisest of the Greeks at the siege of Troy

push-pin: a children's game

Timon: an Athenian, the subject of Shakespeare's own *Timon of Athens*, and a famous misanthropist

idle toys: trifles, things of no account

caudle: a drink for invalids. The Folio reading is 'candle', and if accepted suggests that Berowne is offering to help look for their pain

moon-like: changeable, inconstant

Joan: an ordinary girl, as opposed to a fine lady

pruning me: preening myself, improving my appearance to find favour with the women

gait: way of walking

state: way of standing

post: speed

present: something presented, in this case the letter

mar: spoil, harm

Dun Adramadio: Costard's attempt at 'Don Armado'

whoreson loggerhead: wretched block-head

mess: a party of four dining together

pick-purses in love: criminal lovers

turtles: turtle-doves, faithful lovers

cross the cause why we were born: deny those desires that were responsible for bringing us into the world

of all hands: on every side

rent: torn

man of Inde: Indian, who worships the rising sun

strooken: struck

peremptory: arrogant

eagle-sighted: eagles were believed able to look straight into the sun

fury: madness

cull'd sovereignty: chosen best

as at a fair: competitions bringing together the most beautiful girls were perhaps among the entertainment at fairs

several worthies make one dignity: individual good points combine to form a harmonious excellence

wants: is lacking

want: desire

Fie, painted rhetoric: on second thoughts, he sees she needs no praise; her beauty commends itself

Praise too short doth blot: praise, inevitably inadequate, can only spoil the effect

varnish: lend freshness to, like a coat of paint

gives the crutch the cradle's infancy: make the old on crutches feel as young as infants

black as ebony: Rosaline is unfashionably dark, like the 'Dark Lady' of the sonnets

a book: the Bible to swear on

O paradox: calling a dark beauty fair

badge: emblem, identifying mark

the school of night: the source of endless editorial conjecture, some of it seeing a reference to George Chapman's *Shadow of Night* (1594) and the literary circle surrounding Sir Walter Raleigh

beauty's crest becomes the heavens well: another obscure line. At line 242 Berowne speaks of his love as the sun, but, the King argues, her colouring is rather that of night and hell. Only true, or fair, beauty is appropriate to the heavens

Devils soonest tempt: conventionally fair beauty may be deceptive, as devils often take the shape of angels

deck'd: dressed, covered

favour: face

painting: cosmetics. Typical red and white complexions are so often false nowadays that to avoid the suspicion beauties naturally fair paint themselves dark

To look like her are chimney-sweepers black: Dumain ironically dismisses Berowne's claim that others strive to imitate his love

crack: boast

dark is light: besotted by love, Berowne is prepared to call black white

I'll find a fairer face not wash'd today: even an unwashed girl looks better than Berowne's Rosaline

doomsday: the Day of Judgement, or the end of the world

No devil: if he is condemned to hell, he will meet no devil there so frightful as Rosaline

my foot and her face see: your love is as black as my shoe

chat: pointless conversation

quillets: subtleties

affection's men-at-arms: love's fighting-men

Have at you: an invitation to battle

And where that you have vow'd to study, lords: this seems awkward and the text may be corrupt, since the whole argument is repeated a few lines later in almost the same words. The general sense is that the lovers have vowed to study but neglected the one book that could really help them, the lessons written in their ladies' eyes

pore: study minutely

ground: foundation

Promethean fire: in the Greek myth fire was stolen from the gods by Prometheus and given to man, so making possible the development of all art and civilisation

nimble spirits in the arteries: the arteries were believed to carry not only blood but vital spirits which performed many of the functions we now account for by the nervous system

long-during: long-lasting

sinewy: muscular

leaden: dull, heavy

fiery numbers: the verses the lovers have been inspired to compose

keep: remain within. Love, unlike other 'slow arts', involves not a laborious accumulation of facts, but a heightening of all the senses, and so is communicated more rapidly

immured: enclosed, shut up

When the suspicious head of theft is stopp'd: when even a thief on the alert for the slightest sound can hear nothing

cockled: having a shell

dainty Bacchus: the god of wine, sometimes a violent spirit, but with a refined palate, though coarse in comparison with the delicate perceptions of the lover

Subtle as Sphinx: ingenious as the sphinx, a mythical monster who destroyed travellers unable to answer the questions she posed

climbing trees in the Hesperides: the eleventh labour of Hercules was to fetch the golden apples guarded by a dragon and watched over by the three daughters of Hesperus, the Hesperides, whose name was sometimes given to the garden where they grew

bright Apollo: Greek god of music and poetry

temper'd: blended

aught: anything

authors: these women were themselves created, or at least fathered, by men

For charity itself fulfills the law: religion commands us to love one another: 'for he that loveth another hath fulfilled the law' (from the Bible, Romans 13:8)

Saint Cupid: wittily bringing together sacred and secular love, and suggested by the King as their battle-cry

Advance your standards: bring forward your flags, continuing the military metaphor

Pell-mell: without maintaining military formation

get the sun of them: be sure to approach so that the sun is behind you and in their eyes, but with a pun on sun and 'son'

lay those glozes by: without any more word-play

attach: take hold of

solace: comfort, entertain

revels: feasts or merry-making

masks: masques, dramatic entertainments involving music and words

Forerun: run before

fitted: provided for, filled with entertainment

'Allons': (*French*) let us go

cockle: darnel, a grass sometimes mistakenly sown instead of corn

justice always whirls in equal measure: justice deals with everyone alike; we cannot expect to be pardoned so easily for breaking our oaths

light wenches: frivolous girls

our copper buys no better treasure: our behaviour does not entitle us to anything better. Copper coins were the least valuable, so 'light wenches' are all that can be expected in return

---

Act V Scene 1

Holofernes, Nathaniel and Dull enter, talking of Armado, whom Holofernes despises for his absurd behaviour and linguistic waywardness.

Armado himself then comes in, with Moth and Costard, who greatly enjoy the high rhetoric which flows when the two men meet. At last Armado comes to the point: the King wishes them to provide some entertainment for the Princess and her ladies. Holofernes suggests the Nine Worthies as an appropriate theme, and they begin to cast the parts. With only five actors there will have to be some doubling, and Holofernes volunteers to play three of the worthies himself, while Dull offers to accompany them on the drum.

NOTES AND GLOSSARY:

Holofernes's objections to Armado's misuse of language are full of irony, since he if anyone draws out 'the thread of his verbosity finer than the staple of his argument' (lines 16–17). Holofernes is a pedant, struggling like the old grammarians to resist change and make English conform with Latin. Armado is equally out of touch, following yesterday's rhetorical fashions. As they discover in this scene, they have more in common than they had suspected, though neither has the wit or linguisitic invention of the boy Moth.

'Satis quid sufficit':	(*Latin*) enough is as good as a feast
reasons:	reasoning, conversation
sententious:	full of good sense
scurrility:	indecency
affection:	affectation
without opinion:	without being opinionated
strange:	original
quondam:	previous
intituled:	entitled, called
'Novi hominem tanquam te':	(*Latin*) I know the man as well as I know you
humour:	temperament
lofty:	haughty
filed:	polished
thrasonical:	boastful
picked:	over-refined
spruce:	over-elegant
peregrinate:	like a traveller who has picked up foreign manners
singular:	without equal
verbosity:	wordiness
staple:	the fibre of wool. The metaphor, derived from spinning, suggests that Armado stretches out his sentences more than the substance will bear
insociable:	unbearable
point-devise:	over-precise

rackers of orthography: those whose pronunciation wrenches words from the way they are written as the rack, an instrument of torture, distorts the limbs of its victims

clepeth: old word for 'calls'. Time was not on Holfernes's side, and the pronunciations he objects to are now standard

'vocatur': (*Latin*) is called

it insinuateth me of insanie: it suggests insanity to me

ne intelligis domine: (*Latin*) do you understand, sir?

'Laus Deo, bone intelligo': (*Latin*) praise God, I understand well

'Bone? Bon, fort bon': Holofernes questions Nathaniel's Latin, expecting 'bene' for well, and translates it into French, 'very good'. Throughout the play there are inaccuracies in the Latin, though it is now difficult to tell whether they were intended by Shakespeare or the result of printers' errors

Priscian: Roman grammarian active early in the sixth century AD. Nathaniel's Latin grammar, though still serviceable, is in need of repair

'Videsne quis venit': (*Latin*) do you see who is coming?

'Video, et gaudeo': (*Latin*) I see and am glad

Chirrah: a variant of 'sirrah', presumably addressed to Moth. Commentators have seen a reference to Raleigh's West Country accent or a failed attempt at 'chaere', a Greek salutation

'Quare': (*Latin*) why

well encountered: I am happy to meet you

The alms basket of words: left-overs from a feast might be saved as alms for the poor

honorificabilitudinitatibus: the length is more important than the meaning, though it is a variant of 'honourableness'

flap-dragon: plum or raisin floating in ignited liquor, swallowed in a Christmas game

peal: usually the sound of bells

letter'd: a man of letters

horn-book: book with a protective covering of transparent horn from which schoolboys learnt the rudiments of spelling

Ba: sound made by sheep

'pueritia': (*Latin*) boyhood

'Quis': (*Latin*) who?

consonant: a nothing without the sound of a vowel added

quick venue: quick riposte, a thrust in (verbal) fencing

home: striking the target, again from swordplay

The last of the five vowels: 'u' or 'you', Moth's answer to Armado's question 'who is a sheep?'. The Spanish word for sheep, 'oueia', was apparently used to help boys remember the five vowels, which gives the fooling an extra point

wit-old: wittol, or cuckold

the figure: figure of speech, point of the allusion

Horns: the mark of the cuckold

whip thy gig: play with your top

'manu cita': (*Latin*) with a swift hand, if this is the correct reading. The Quarto prints the incomprehensible 'unu cita'

gingerbread: a kind of cake

pigeon-egg: small but good, like Moth

discretion: wisdom

ad dunghill: comic mistake for the Latin *ad unguem*, 'to a nail', exactly. A dunghill is a heap of manure, hence Holofernes' 'I smell false Latin'

Arts-man: scholar

preambulate: walk ahead, to avoid the uncouth Costard

charge-house: the sense implies a school, though the word is not known elsewhere. Presumably a school where a charge or fee was paid

mons, the hill: Holofernes finds 'hill' better than mountain as a translation of the Latin 'mons'

sans: without

affection: desire

congratulate: greet

The posteriors of the day: since posteriors also means 'buttocks', Armado's term would certainly amuse the 'rude multitude', though as the Latin for 'latter parts' it appeals to Holofernes

liable: admissable

congruent: appropriate

measurable: fitting

culled: chosen

familiar: friend

inward: confidential

let it pass: we will say no more about it

remember thy courtesy: Armado reminds Holofernes to remove his hat at the mention of the King's name, and then to put it back on

importunate: pressing, urgent

his grace: the King

excrement:	that which grows out, here his moustache
I recount no fable:	I'm not inventing all this
the very all of all:	what it adds up to
chuck:	term of endearment
antic:	grotesque entertainment
the Nine Worthies:	nine great men of history, including classical, biblical and courtly examples. There were some variations, and Hercules and Pompey were not usually part of the list
illustrate:	illustrious
Joshua:	leader of the Israelites after the death of Moses, remembered for his destruction of the city of Jericho
myself and this gallant gentleman:	the text must be corrupt here, as only one part is given to Nathaniel ('this gallant gentleman') and Holofernes. In fact most of the parts are differently assigned when we get to the pageant itself
Judas Maccabaeus:	leader of an Israelite rebellion for religious freedom against the emperor Antiochus. He died in battle in 160 BC
Pompey the Great:	Roman general (106–48 BC) eventually defeated by Julius Caesar
in minority:	as a child. Hercules first showed signs of his great strength when still in the cradle by strangling two snakes sent by the jealous Juno. He was the child of her husband by Alcmene of Argolis
if any of the audience hiss:	hissing was a way of expressing disapproval, but if snakes are involved Moth suggests it can be passed off as part of the sound-effects
fadge:	succeed
Via:	come along
tabor:	small drum, usually accompanying the pipe
hay:	country dance
Most dull:	Holofernes does not think much of Dull's offer

Act V Scene 2

The Princess and her ladies discuss the presents and verses they have received from the King and his friends. Suspicious of this sudden change of heart after their inhospitable welcome, they decide to mock them, and see the opportunity when Boyet enters. He has overheard the King and the others rehearsing an entertainment in which they will appear before the Princess disguised as Muscovites. They plan to approach their respective ladies, identifying them by the favours or rosettes they have sent. To prevent this the ladies exchange favours and agree to be as uncooperative as possible when their lovers arrive. They ridicule the Muscovites and refuse to dance, though they allow the King and his men to profess their love, though not to the ladies they imagine. Admitting defeat the men go out, to return without their disguises, apologising for not coming sooner. The ladies now complain of the foolish Muscovites, pretending not to realise that they and the King's friends are the same. Beaten again, Berowne suggests they confess everything and make the best of it. They have broken one oath, but will not be forsworn again. The ladies now hold them to the promises they made, unknowingly, to the wrong women, misled by the exchange of favours, and again the men get the worst of it. Costard then comes to announce the pageant of the Nine Worthies. The others follow in their turn, though the King and his friends relieve their own wounded pride by mocking the performance until it disintegrates, with Costard and Armado about to come to blows.

At this point Marcade, a messenger, enters with news that the Princess's father is dead. She must leave at once, though the men again urge their love. The ladies agree to listen in a year's time, but meanwhile they must renounce the pleasures of the world more effectively than at their last attempt. Armado comes to take his leave with Jaquenetta who has imposed a penance on him, so that he has to prove his reformation by working on the land for three years. Finally Holofernes and Nathaniel return with a dialogue between the owl and the cuckoo, representing winter and spring, which concludes the play.

NOTES AND GLOSSARY:
Entertainments like the masque of Muscovites were often held at great houses or the inns of court, and a Christmas Revels at Gray's Inn in 1594 included a similar masque which Shakespeare may have seen, since his own *Comedy of Errors* was part of the programme. This fact perhaps helps to date the play, though contacts with Russia were becoming more frequent in the 1580s and 1590s.

Throughout the scene the ladies act to punish and chasten the men for their presumption in setting themselves apart from the world, and to demonstrate that their famous wit is easily defeated. Led by Berowne the men try for a new sincerity, though it is difficult to shake off old habits, and enforced contact with the less attractive aspects of life must precede their marriage to the ladies. The sudden news of the King's death appropriately breaks off the rather cruel mirth at the honest efforts of Holofernes and his friends, and chimes with the penance decreed by Rosaline for Berowne, twelve months to be spent in hospitals visiting the sick.

The songs of the owl and the cuckoo, the finest poetry in the play, remind us of nature and the seasons, a world more profound and more permanent than the whims of Navarre and his book-men or the affectations of pedants and courtiers.

fairings: presents, originally those purchased at fairs

A lady wall'd about with diamonds: describing a piece of jewellery sent by the King

margent: margin

fain: pleased

wax: grow larger, punning on the wax with which the letter is sealed with a representation of the boy Cupid

shrewd unhappy gallows: curst unlucky villain, or gallows bird, deserving to be hanged

grandam: grandmother

dark: hidden

mouse: term of endearment

taking it in snuff: being offended by it, as by the smell of a candle snuffed out

Look what you do, you do it still i' th' dark: whatever you do, you do it secretly

I weigh not you: I'm not as heavy as you, but Rosaline takes it to mean 'I attach no weight to your opinion'

past care is still past cure: usually what is past cure is past care, it is no use troubling about what cannot be remedied

Well bandied: a witty exchange of words. The term derives from a game like tennis where the ball went from one player to another

favour: rosette, love-token, but punning on favour as 'face' and at line 33 as 'attractiveness'

numbering: calculation

fairs: fair ladies

Much in the letters, nothing in the praise: the black ink of the letters matches her colour, but Rosaline modestly rejects the praise

a text B: elaborately inked letter B, perhaps prompted by 'Beauteous' in the previous line

Ware pencils: beware of pencils, suggesting that Katharine relies too much on cosmetics

let me not die your debtor: I must pay you back for that remark

dominical: the red letter S denoting Sunday in old calendars

golden: like red referring to Katharine's amber hair

full of O's: marks caused by chicken-pox or small-pox

beshrew all shrows: curse all shrews. The Princess interrupts their sniping at each other

twain:	two
to purchase:	to buy it with their presents
in by the week:	caught fast, perhaps referring to some form of prison sentence
fawn:	cringe like a dog looking for attention
bootless:	useless
hests:	behests, commands
to make me proud that jests:	to please me when in fact I am only joking
Pair-Taunt:	the winning hand in an obsolete card-game
his fate:	the destiny he cannot escape
in wisdom hatch'd:	born of wisdom. Such folly has the ingenuity to show itself on a grand scale
note:	stigma, black mark
To prove, by wit, worth in simplicity:	all the wise man's skill is perverted in trying to demonstrate the value of his folly
Saint Denis to Saint Cupid:	answering one battle-cry with another. St Denis is patron saint of France
scout:	Boyet goes ahead like a military scout to look out for danger
neighbour:	nearby
knavish:	mischievous
conn'd:	learnt
embassage:	errand
ever and anon:	now and again
made a doubt:	expressed a fear
Presence majestical:	the royal presence of the Princess
put him out:	make him forget his lines
wag:	joker
fleer'd:	grinned
with his finger and thumb:	snapping his fingers with enthusiasm
caper'd:	danced
turn'd on the toe:	spun round to leave
zealous:	whole-hearted
this spleen:	the organ thought to regulate violent emotions. They laugh until they cry
Muscovites:	natives of Moscow
parle:	talk
love-feat:	love-suit makes sense, and the word here may be a misprint
gallants:	lovers, men of fashion
Despite of suit:	in spite of asking
most in sight:	where they can easily be seen
mock for mock:	to answer mockery with mockery
counsels:	declarations of love

unbosom:	reveal, confess
visages:	faces
to the death:	if we die for it
penn'd speech:	specially composed, not spontaneous
n'er come in:	never take up their parts
intended game:	perhaps on the evidence of Boyet's report she does not believe that the men are serious in their professions of love
Blackamoors:	African negroes, rather incongruously part of the Muscovite entertainment
visored:	masked
taffeta:	the ladies' taffeta masks are all that Moth can see
holy parcel:	divine group
'out' indeed:	Boyet takes him to mean 'out of his part', forgetting his lines
vouchsafe:	condescend to
perfectness:	competence in remembering his lines
measur'd:	travelled, though Rosaline takes them to mean 'calculated the distance'
measure:	dance
still without account:	without ever counting the cost or trouble
clouded:	referring to the mask she wears
eyne:	eyes
one change:	one figure or round of the dance
not strange:	clear enough, with nothing foreign about it
the man:	the man in the moon
nice:	over-fastidious
Court'sy:	at the end of the dance the ladies would curtsey to the men
Price you yourselves:	name your own price
two treys:	two threes at dice. He matches her three sweet words with three more
Metheglin:	Welsh drink containing honey
wort:	unfermented beer
malmsey:	a sweet wine
Seventh sweet:	Berowne himself
cog:	cheat, especially at dice
Thou griev'st my gall:	you rub me where I am already sore. Gall was also the bitter fluid found in the gall-bladder, hence Rosaline's reply
meet:	appropriate, because not sweet
change a word:	hold a conversation, but Maria takes him literally and gives him 'Fair lord' in exchange for his 'Fair lady'

without a tongue:	masks were kept in place by a leather tongue held in the mouth. Katharine finds that Longaville has little to say for himself
a double tongue:	perhaps because Katharine is so ready with words, or because she has a forked, or deceitful, tongue
Veal:	Dutch pronunciation of 'well' or the Dutch word for 'plenty', punning on the second half of Longaville's name, and on 'veil' or mask. Veal, as she says, is also the meat of the calf, and calf another term for fool
part:	divide and share
your half:	your better-half or wife
ox:	fool
give horns:	cuckold me
Bleat:	sound made by sheep and calves
Above the sense of sense:	too fine for common perception
sensible:	perceptive, effective
conference:	conversation
conceits:	conceptions
dry-beaten:	bruised, though no blood is drawn
pure scoff:	simple mockery
breed:	species, race
Tapers:	candles
well-liking:	plump and inactive
kingly-poor flout:	a poor attempt to mock us, with a quibble on Rosaline's 'well-liking'
pert:	lively, bold
lamentable cases:	sad condition, punning on 'cases' as masks
weeping-ripe:	ready to weep
out of all suit:	beyond all reason, punning on 'suit' as wooing
'No point':	(corrupted *French*) not at all. There is punning on the point of the sword
came o'er:	overcame, conquered
trow you:	do you know
Qualm:	feeling of nausea or misgiving
statute-caps:	woollen caps which apprentices were obliged by statute to wear. Simple tradesmen are wittier than these lords, Rosaline declares
digest:	swallow, endure
repair:	return
blow:	blossom
damask:	red and white
commixture:	complexion
vailing:	lowering, so that they no longer hide their beauty

Avaunt perplexity: enough of these puzzles (as the masks are removed)
gear: dress
rough carriage: uncouth behaviour
whip: move quickly
roes: female deer
proper habits: own clothes
pease: peas
wakes: local holidays
wassails: revels involving drinking
we that sell by gross: those of us with a large stock of wit are less accomplished at showing it off than insubstantial characters like Boyet
pins the wenches on his sleeve: has all the girls after him
carve: use elaborate and affected gestures
lisp: speak in the same way
ape: imitator
monsieur the nice: a really fastidious gentleman. Such affectations were usually blamed on the French
mean: middle or tenor part, punning on mean as poor, undistinguished
ushering: leading in with a proper show of respect
Mend: improve
as whale his bone: as whalebone
this madman: Boyet, whose extravagances spell the ruin of natural manners
All hail: a salutation, but the Princess takes hail as hailstones, and so foul weather
virtue: power
nickname: name wrongly
virtue's office: the exercise of virtue, here meaning goodness
mess: party of four
talk'd apace: chattered away
fools would fain have drink: fools desire to drink (so that 'they' and 'fools' are identical)
dry: not amusing
By light we lose light: the light of the sun blinds us
what doth to you belong: the name of fool
superfluous case: unnecessary mask
described: recognised
face of brass: shamelessness
Taffeta phrases: showy but insubtantial rhetoric
three pil'd hyperboles: richly exaggerated expressions. Three-piled velvet was the thickest
russet: brown, like the clothes of simple country people

blown me full of maggot ostentation: made me swollen with pretentious-
ness, 'maggot' being both the larva of insects and a
whimsical idea or obsession

kersey: coarse woollen cloth

Wench: term for country girl rather than a lady, announcing
Berowne's new plain-speaking

sans: without, a French affectation which Rosaline
rejects

the old rage: my former insanity

Lord have mercy: an inscription used to mark houses visited by the
plague

tokens: plague spots, punning on the favours which the
ladies are wearing

free: not really in love

Our states are forfeit: everything we have is lost

being those that sue: Rosaline understands 'sue' not as 'pay court to'
but as 'prosecute in law'. Therefore they cannot be
the defendants as they claim

well advis'd: aware of what you were doing

force not: value not

remit: give up

consent: agreement, conspiracy

dash: spoil

carry-tale: tale-bearer

please-man: yes-man, sycophant

zany: buffoon

trencher-knight: one better at eating than fighting

Dick: fellow

smiles his cheek in years: his face wrinkled with laughter

but the sign of she: only the semblance of the lady

in will and error: deliberately but mistakenly

Much upon this 'tis: this is how it must have been

by the square: to the inch. Boyet is on intimate terms with the
Princess, and knows how to please

the apple of her eye: her pupil. Face to face at close range is the meaning
of the whole phrase

trencher: dish

allow'd: permitted, like a licensed jester

smock: a woman's dress, alluding to his effeminacy or hinting that women will be the death of him

leaden sword: one with no cutting edge

manage: practice gallop, a term from the riding-school

career: rapid movement of a horse and rider

tilting: offering to fight, thrusting with a lance

straight:	straightaway, immediately
pure wit:	unaffected wit, in contrast to Boyet's
fray:	fight
vara:	dialect for 'very'
pursents:	presents, represents
under correction:	tell me if I am wrong
beg us:	fool us

whereuntil it doth amount: what it adds up to. It is difficult to see why Berowne and Costard disagree, unless Costard wishes to say that what they are offering cannot be reckoned in terms of simple arithmetic

parfect:	perfect, play
Pompion:	pumpkin, Costard's substitution for Pompey
degree:	rank or standing
turn it finely off:	make a success of it
'tis some policy:	it is a wise plan
contents:	subject-matter

Dies in the zeal of that which it presents: collapses because of the over-enthusiasm of the actor

our sport:	the masque of Muscovites
Anointed:	at his coronation the king is anointed

a man of God's making: an ordinary human being

That is all one:	that does not matter
fortuna de la guerra:	(*Italian*) the fortune of war
couplement:	couple
Hector of Troy:	noblest of the Trojan princes killed at the siege of Troy
Alexander:	Alexander the Great (356–323BC), King of Macedonia, brilliant general and founder of Alexandria
thrive:	succeed
habits:	costumes
hedge-priest:	country parson with no church of his own

Abate throw at novum: except for the throw at novem quinque, 'nine-five', a dice game; playing on the numbers involved in the pageant

in his vein:	in his particular style
The ship is under sail:	the show is under way
amain:	at full speed
libbard's head:	leopard's or lion's head, Pompey's coat-of-arms, perhaps displaced as Costard stumbles on entering, so providing an opportunity for the witticisms of Berowne and Boyet, who here bury their differences
targe:	small shield
scutcheon:	escutcheon, coat-of-arms

too right:	Alexander was described as holding his head inclined to the left
tender-smelling:	Alexander was also known for his sweet-smelling skin. Here Boyet smells the difference between the hero and the hedge-priest
the painted cloth:	a canvas painted with the Nine Worthies, a popular subject for wall decorations. Costard says that Alexander (as impersonated by Nathaniel) will be demoted and his place given to Ajax, punning on 'a jakes', a lavatory, a common quibble of the period
poll-axe:	battle axe
close-stool:	commode
dashed:	dismayed, embarrassed
o'erparted:	given a role too difficult for him
Cerberus:	three-headed dog guarding the entrance to the Greek underworld. The final labour of Hercules was to capture this animal
'canus':	properly 'canis', Latin for dog
'manus':	(*Latin*) hand
'Quoniam':	(*Latin*) because
'Ergo':	(*Latin*) therefore
Keep some state:	maintain some dignity
Iscariot:	Judas Iscariot, the disciple who betrayed Jesus Christ, identifying him to the officers of the chief priests with a kiss. Overcome with remorse, he later hanged himself, traditionally from an elder tree
ycleped:	called, but punning on 'clipt', shortened. To clip was also to kiss, providing Berowne with his next pun
You are my elder:	Holofernes defers to Boyet as his senior
out of countenance:	made to look ashamed. 'Countenance' means face, hence Berowne's reply
cittern-head:	carved head of a guitar-like instrument
bodkin:	hair pin, often elaborately carved
death's face in a ring:	death's head rings, engraved with the Latin words *memento mori*, remember you must die, were common at the time
scarce seen:	almost obliterated by time
pommel:	knob of sword handle
falchion:	sword
Saint George:	patron saint of England, and so often carved on brooches 'half-cheek' or in profile

toothdrawer: dentist, identified by the badge worn in his cap

put thee in countenance: restored your confidence, and given you a face

An thou wert a lion: even if Holofernes were a lion, they would refuse to be overawed by him

not humble: arrogant

baited: harassed, teased

Hide thy head, Achilles: champion of the Greeks as Hector was of the Trojans. He treacherously killed Hector at the siege of Troy

but a Trojan: an ordinary Trojan

clean-timbered: well-built

calf: part of the leg, but punning on 'calf' or fool

indued: endowed, gifted

small: part of the leg below the calf

makes faces: creates faces, but also grimmaces

armipotent: mighty in arms

Mars: the god of war in classical mythology

A gilt nutmeg: a nutmeg glazed with egg-white and used to flavour wine like the lemon with cloves; a common lover's gift but incongruous for Mars or Hector

cloven: punning on the aromatic clove to allude to the devil's cloven hoof

heir of Ilion: Hector, as eldest son of King Priam, was heir of Ilion or Troy

so breath'd: never short of breath

that flower: that flower of chivalry he would say, if he was not interrupted with the names of common flowers

rein: control

give it the rein: allow to run free

Hector's a greyhound: Hector was a common name for hounds

forward with my device: go on with my speech

yard: three feet, but also slang for penis

Hannibal: Carthaginian general (c.247–183BC) who crossed the Alps in an unsuccessful attempt to capture Rome

The party is gone: the man, Hector, is dead, but Costard takes up 'gone' in the colloquial sense of 'pregnant', and refers it to Jaquenetta

honest Trojan: good fellow. The term survives in the modern expression 'to work like a Trojan'. Unless Armado marries Jaquenetta, her reputation will be lost

quick: with child

infamonize: infamise, defame

sup: feed

Ates: spirits of discord in Greek mythology, from the name of one of Jupiter's daughters

northern man: a favourite weapon of the lawless Scots was a long staff or pole

bepray: beg, ask

uncasing: taking off his doublet

bloods: gallants, men of spirit

woolward for penance: wearing only woollen outer clothes, lacking a linen shirt. As a form of penance voluntary discomfort was sometimes practised, but Armado simply cannot afford garments not usually seen

in Rome: a place of pilgrimage as the seat of the church

dishclout: dishcloth

I have seen the day of wrong through the little hole of discretion: to see day at a little hole was proverbial for 'to see the light', to understand clearly. Armado now recognises his wrongdoing and will behave more wisely in future

new-sad soul: soul newly made sad or serious

liberal opposition: the freedom with which we have opposed you

converse of breath: conversation

gentleness: kindness, forbearance

humble: sufficiently polite

my great suit: presumably the mission that brought her to Navarre, now happily settled

The extreme parts of time: when time is running out, everything is brought to a head of necessity, and often settled at once where longer discussion had failed

at his very loose: a term from archery, at the critical moment, when the bow-string is released

progeny: filial descent. The Princess must mourn her father, and the King cannot press his suit

convince: prove, demonstrate

first on foot: already under way

justle: jostle, push aside

wholesome-profitable: good for the health

double: at the loss of a father and at parting from friends 'newly found'

badges: signs or symbols, the words which are inevitably inadequate to the occasion, or perhaps the favours and presents the King has sent

Play'd foul play with: broken

deform'd: corrupted

unbefitting strains: inappropriate or unseemly tendencies

party-coated:	motley, the dress of fools
misbecom'd:	not suited with. Berowne apologises for their clownish behaviour which in the ladies' eyes has made them appear less serious than they are
ambassadors:	messengers
maiden council:	the ladies discussing the matter amongst themselves
bombast:	stuffing to pad clothes, rather than real substance
lining:	again, something to fill out the time
devout:	serious
in our respects:	as regarding you
quote:	reckon, account
dear guiltiness:	serious culpability, though there may be a pun as the reason for his perjury no doubt endears him to the Princess
as there is no such cause:	though you are not obliged to
naked:	unfurnished
twelve celestial signs:	the signs of the zodiac, marking the twelve months of the year
insociable:	solitary
weeds:	clothes
last love:	survive as love
this virgin palm now kissing thine:	she takes his hand as she speaks
intitled:	having a claim
to flatter up these powers of mine with rest:	to indulge my senses with idleness
Hence hermit:	henceforward I shall be a hermit
to your sins are racked:	until your sins are wrung from you
attaint:	dishonoured
smooth-faced:	plausible, and also without a beard
The liker you:	the more like you, again punning on Longaville's name and height and perhaps suggesting that it will give him time to grow up
Studies my lady:	Rosaline is thinking before she decides his penance
replete with mocks:	full of mockery
all estates:	people of all kinds
wormwood:	a bitter herb, spoiling the flavour of Berowne's wit
loose grace:	casual, easily-won favour
prosperity:	success
Jack hath not his Jill:	the negative form of a proverbial expression of the traditional 'happy ending'
a comedy:	a play ending happily
votary:	one vowed to serve
Holla:	a shout to excite attention
pied:	of two or more colours

lady-smocks . . . cuckoo-buds: flowers apparently discovered by Shakespeare in the pages of Gerard's *Herball* (1597), in which case the songs are later than most of the play

cuckoo: traditionally unlucky, and for its similarity to the word 'cuckold', especially 'unpleasing to a married ear'

oaten straws: pipes made from oat straws

ploughman's clocks: the skylark is traditionally an early riser, like the ploughman

tread: mate

daws: jackdaws

blows his nail: whiles away his time as the season gives him no work to do, though the sense of blowing on the fingers to warm them may be present too

pail: bucket

ways be foul: roads are muddy

greasy Joan: the kitchen maid, cooling or 'keeling' the pot on the fire to prevent it boiling over

saw: wise saying

crabs: crab-apples

Mercury: messenger of the Greek gods, less musical than Apollo. The status of the sentence is uncertain, but it is probably spoken by Armado. In the Folio there is an additional line 'You that way: we this way', again perhaps spoken by Armado before he and Jaquenetta leave, or before the men and the French ladies separate.

Part 3

Commentary

The title

Though Charles Gildon in his edition of *Shakespeare's Life and Works* (1710) writes that he 'can't well tell why the Author gave this Play this name' there is no real difficulty. In spite of all their labours, the lovers are unable to persuade the ladies of the seriousness of their intentions before Marcade arrives with the news that breaks off the wooing. Some critics doubt if they ever will be successful, but comic convention surely leaves us to hope that in a year and a day all will be well.

While Shakespeare's tragedies and histories name the principal character in their title, in his comedies, where the group counts for more than any individual, he usually suggests the theme or mood of the play. *Much Ado About Nothing*, *As You Like It*, and *All's Well That Ends Well* are other examples.

The play's subtitle, 'a pleasant conceited comedy', indicates the ingenious and fanciful turns which make up the plot.

The sources

This is the only play of Shakespeare with no known literary source. Attempts have been made to link the Princess's visit with royal embassies to the King of Navarre in 1578 and 1586, when among the nobles at court were names which coincide with those of some of the characters in the play. But if Shakespeare was rewriting some earlier play with topical references to either of these visits, the traces are too faint to detain us. Suggestions that there are allusions to contemporary figures like Raleigh, Harvey and Nashe, already mentioned in Part 1 of these notes, are much more convincing. No doubt these were enjoyed by the first audiences, but they are lost to us; and yet the play survives.

Shakespeare may have had no single source, but he started writing with inherited ideas on the nature of comedy. As C. L. Barber shows in *Shakespeare's Festive Comedy* (1959), without the May-games and holidays of Shakespeare's childhood, and without the ceremonies and revels which accompanied the Queen's summer progress when the court removed from London, *Love's Labour's Lost* could not have been the kind of play it is. We can also trace the influence of the Commedia dell'Arte, a form of improvised entertainment involving stock characters, originating in Italy in the early sixteenth century and spreading all over Europe. These prototypes are visible behind most of the characters below the level of the nobility, and in the stage directions and speech headings of the Quarto they show through when Holofernes is called simply 'Pedant' and Armado 'Braggart'.

Whatever his sources, even in this early play the result is unmistakably Shakespeare's.

Critical history

The play was revived during the reign of James I but soon passed into obscurity. During the seventeenth century, critics came to require a literary decorum which left no room for the exuberance and extravagance so often found in Shakespeare. The pun, in which *Love's Labour's Lost* abounds, was particularly despised, and writing in the *Spectator* in 1714, Joseph Addison (1672-1719), complained that the seeds of punning 'though they may be subdued by reason, reflection, and good sense, they will be very apt to shoot up in the greatest genius, that is not broken and cultivated by the rules of art'. John Dryden (1631-1700), in *A Defence of the Epilogue* (1672), had already classed our play among those 'either grounded on impossibilities, or at least, so meanly written, that the comedy neither caus'd your mirth, nor the serious part your concernment'. Charles Gildon in his *Shakespeare's Life and Works* (1710) thought it Shakespeare's very worst play, but unlike some scholars of the time, was at least prepared to believe that Shakespeare had written it. Fifty years later, Dr Johnson (1709-1784), rereading the play for his edition of Shakespeare (1765), found 'many passages mean, childish and vulgar; and some which ought not to have been exhibited, as we are told they were, to a maiden queen. But there are scattered through the whole, many sparks of genius; nor is there any play that has more evident marks of the hand of Shakespeare'.

The beginnings of the romantic movement in literature brought more sympathetic attitudes, though William Hazlitt (1778-1830), could still begin his remarks on *Love's Labour's Lost* in the *Characters of Shakespeare's Plays* (1817) by saying 'If we were to part with any of the author's comedies, it should be this'. But he found much to admire in the play, and in Shakespeare's comic genius: 'It has little satire and no spleen. It aims at the ludicrous rather than the ridiculous. It makes us laugh at the follies of mankind, not despise them, and still less bear any ill-will towards them'. S. T. Coleridge (1772-1834), believing it, in his *Notes on the Comedies* (1818), the earliest of the plays, recognised many of Shakespeare's features 'tho' as in a portrait taken of him in his boyhood'. He was interested in 'the wonderful activity of thought' and in the whimsical language of the play, reflecting a time 'when men of rank and fashion affected a display of wit, point, and sententious observation, that would be deemed intolerable at present'. Coleridge was influenced by those German critics who were among the first to understand Shakespeare's greatness, and another of them, G. G. Gervinus (1805–71), in *Shakespeare Commentaries* (1849–50), saw even in the comedies the author's concern with serious moral issues, *Love's Labour's Lost* centring on 'a vain desire of fame in all its forms':

> The King has chosen Armado to amuse them by his minstrelsy during their hermit-life; and similar to the contempt with which the King regards his boasting vein is the scorn with which Biron views the learned and ascetic vanity of the King; but he himself has fallen into a still higher vanity, for which he incurs Rosaline's censure.

In England, Walter Pater (1839–94) was less given to moralising than most Victorian literary men, though he shared the age's taste for impressionistic, biographical criticism. In his *Appreciations* (1889), this more flexible approach shows in his account of *Love's Labour's Lost*:

> the unity of the play is not so much the unity of a drama as that of a series of pictorial groups, in which the same figures reappear, in different combinations but on the same background. It is as if Shakespeare had intended to bind together, by some inventive conceit, the devices of an ancient tapestry, and give voices to its figures, . . . It is this foppery of delicate language, this fashionable plaything of his time, with which Shakespeare is occupied in *Love's Labour's Lost*.

In the Victorian period the play returned to the stage, after an absence of two hundred years, and in the present century there have been many successful revivals. In his *Prefaces to Shakespeare* (1927) Granville-Barker (1877–1946), is concerned with the problems of producing a play 'five-sixths of it, more decorative exercise than drama', though alive everywhere with evidence of Shakespeare's craftsmanship. 'The whole play, first and last, demands style', he rightly says, and while scholars have exhaustively examined the historical sources and topical allusions, others have attempted to define and illustrate this style. In his influential book, *Shakespeare's Festive Comedy* (1959), C. L. Barber relates the play to underlying Saturnalian patterns it shares with Elizabethan holidays and May-games, where release leads to clarification. Perhaps the best single essay on *Love's Labour's Lost* was written by Bobbyann Roesen in 1953 for *Shakespeare Quarterly*, while she was still a student at Bryn Mawr College.

The characters

We do not expect the characters in a comedy to have the formative role which has made 'character in action' a definition of plot. Holofernes and Armado have the sharp outlines of caricature, but most of the others, though gifted with memorably individual phrases, have no more reality than is required for the author's purposes. If we find it strange that Berowne in the first scene should point out the defects of the King's statutes and yet subscribe to them himself, we should not look to realistic psychology for an explanation.

King Ferdinand of Navarre

His title gives him precedence, and the fashionable ambition to make the court a 'little academe' is his also, but for the most part he is content to leave the initiative to Berowne. There is no suggestion that he has more poetic ability than his peers, and Marcade's arrival leaves him searching in vain for terms to tell his love.

Dumain and Longaville

Granville-Barker grants them 'about the substance of echoes', but the producer must make some distinction. Most of the relevant information comes in Act II Scene 1, where the ladies remember earlier meetings. Longaville seems the more forceful of the two. Maria describes his 'sharp wit match'd with too blunt a will' (line 49); he it was who devised the 'dread penalty' (I.1.126) prescribing the loss of her tongue for any woman coming within a mile of the court; and who loses his temper with Boyet (II.1.202). His height is punningly connected with his name in the final scene, where Dumain's lack of a beard rouses Katharine's comment. Dumain's sonnet is in a simpler, more pastoral vein than Longaville's offering and its tangled rhetoric. Yet both mock the Worthies just as harshly, and are essentially elegant, witty, and inexperienced young noblemen.

Berowne

He is the play's hero, though E. M. W. Tillyard finds him 'a mouth rather than a formed character'. Much of his relative complexity springs from the fact that he is both a participant in the action and a commentator on it. This dual role has often attracted comment, and Muriel Bradbrook writes that he 'runs with the hare and hunts with the hounds'.* The hostile critic of love who finds himself in love against his

*Shakespeare and Elizabethan Poetry, Chatto and Windus, London, 1951.

will is familiar in comedy, but Berowne seems a willing participant even while one part of his mind resists. Even his love for Rosaline shows the same ambivalence, where at one moment he maligns her character and behaviour and at the next leaps to her defence against the more orthodox beauties admired by his friends. His mixed feelings are relevant both to the urge to found the academy, and to its inevitable defeat, since love is a supreme instance of those natural processes which are one aspect of 'cormorant devouring Time' (I.1.4). Berowne's 'Promethean fire' speech in ACT IV Scene 3 idealises irresistibly the positive side of these same processes, sweeping away the doubts of his friends, but the scene leaves him aware that reality cannot so easily be dispelled by his mock-logic:

> Light wenches may prove plagues to men forsworn;
> If so, our copper buys no better treasure.   (IV.3.381–2)

Capable of this degree of self-awareness, Berowne is the only character capable of growth, though to the last he retains 'a trick of the old rage' (V.2.416–7), to be purged only by the year's penance.

Boyet

Berowne's characterisation of the French lord in Act V Scene 2 is prompted by his own defeat, but full of Shakespeare's usual amused contempt for this kind of ladies' man. Even the Princess finds Boyet's flattering praise too fulsome, and his language is some of the most artificial in a play rich in elaborate verbal gesture. For all his knowingness he represents no real sexual threat, so the ladies are happy to take him into their confidence.

Marcade

He has the shortest part, but the most impressive entrance. Commentators have connected his name with Mercade, the French form of Mercury, whose words 'are harsh after the songs of Apollo' (V.2.922), and have seen a punning reference to his role as the ghost at the feast, the messenger who 'mars Arcadia'.

Don Adriano de Armado

Holofernes finds 'his general behaviour vain, ridiculous and thrasonical' (V.1.11–12), this last epithet, derived from Thraso, the braggart soldier of Roman comedy, gives us the stock figure which Shakespeare transforms into something much richer. Armado is also a melancholy lover, his desire for Jaquenetta making him absurd but also more human. His reverence for a vanished heroic world is never contemptible, but filled with a pathos which makes us think of another proud but impoverished Spaniard, Don Quixote in the novel by Cervantes (1547–1616), though the first part of *Don Quixote* was not published until 1605. As a man of fashion, Armado prides himself on his social accomplishments, 'the varnish of a complete man' (I.2.40), and his inflated language, seen especially in his two letters, has a bizarre logic deriving from Sidney and the various handbooks of rhetoric from the middle of the century. His reformation is no doubt genuine, and his vow to Jaquenetta 'to hold the plough for her sweet love three year' (V.2.875) represents a closer approach to the realities underlying his earlier world of fantasy, but he will always be an eccentric figure.

Moth

The page's main role is to display the foolishness of his master, though Armado's admiration for his 'sweet smoke of rhetoric' (III.1.60) is among the Spaniard's more endearing characteristics. When Holofernes is present, Moth gives him the same treatment, and one of the pleasures of the play is to see the diminutive Moth running rings round the ponderous pronouncements of the two older men. He has a mental agility which only Berowne among the men can equal, though in the masque of the Muscovites for once we see him put out of his part.

Holofernes

The pedantic schoolmaster has a high opinion of his own gifts, though they do not include the effortless inventiveness on which he prides himself. His epitaph on the pricket is strained and mechanical, mere accretion without imagination. His fondness for synonymy, where he shows off his vocabulary without advancing to a clearer or more striking perception of the object defined, is further evidence of his limitations. He takes his stand on the authority of the Latin authors, and is engaged in an endless battle to prevent the degeneration of the language (as he sees it), threatened alike by Berowne's sonnet and Armado's newfangled pronunciation. Since the battle is a losing one, we feel no animus against him, and in the pageant of the Worthies his reproach to the mocking lords, 'This is not generous, not gentle, not humble' (V.2.623), finds us on his side.

Nathaniel

In the Commedia dell'Arte, the Pedant was often accompanied by a Parasite, and this gives us Nathaniel's role. He is content to echo and compliment his friend, matching his Latin tags and citing his own authorities with half-remembered passages from the Church fathers. And he duly earns his dinner for his pains, at the table of one of the schoolmaster's pupils. But any inclination we have to dismiss him as an oily sycophant is dispelled by Costard's commendation of him after his failure in the pageant: 'a foolish mild man; an honest man, look you, and soon dashed! He is a marvellous good neighbour, faith, and a very good bowler; but for Alisander,—alas! you see how 'tis—a little o'erparted' (V.2.575–79).

Dull

The first of a series of dull Shakespearean constables, culminating in Dogberry in *Much Ado About Nothing*, all of whom share his difficulty with words. He is the only character with no pretentions to wit, his riddle about the moon (IV.2.33) marking his highest aspiration in that direction. He has a certain common sense—as Nathaniel says, he is 'sensible only in the duller parts' (IV.2.26)—and an unexpected and unappreciated talent for the tabor. But his main comic value is to remain silent in a play where all the other characters are unremittingly articulate.

Costard

A busy character, he appears in every scene but one, and is instrumental in various turns of the plot, like the mix-up about the letters, the introduction of the Worthies, and the revelation of Jaquenetta's pregnancy. A rustic clown, his verbal mistakes are more numerous than Dull's, though one suspects that he comically exaggerates his incomprehension for the entertainment of his betters. More significantly, he represents the unregenerate flesh which mocks the pretentions of Navarre's academy.

The Princess of France

In *Love's Labour's Lost* it is the ladies' part to educate the men, and the Princess seems well-fitted for the task. At her first entrance she chides Boyet for burying her true worth with a welter of words, and when the King comes in she is soon correcting him, though quick to apologise:

'But pardon me, I am too sudden-bold:
To teach a teacher ill beseemeth me'   (II.1.106–7).

Many of the women's speeches are interchangeable, but it is noticeable that the Princess at the opening of Act IV seems more self-aware than

Navarre, and that she dominates her followers more effectively than he does. The idea of exchanging favours to confuse the men is hers, though Rosaline devises the additional mockery when the King's men return in their own shapes. During the pageant of the Worthies, her polite encouragement of the amateurs contrasts favourably with the men's often cruel jibes. Her grief at her father's death is formal but unaffected, in comparison with the King's over-elaborate protestations of love, and the penance she prescribes shows a shrewd knowledge of human nature.

Maria and Katherine

Richard David writes of 'the red and gold charm of Katharine, and the brusquer Maria',* but they are no more easily distinguishable than their lovers. The witty exchanges at the opening of Act V Scene 2 give us Katharine's colouring and secretiveness, and more memorably, the death of her sister for love, but all the ladies are equally adept at verbal fencing, and editions are still confused over which lines to ascribe to Katharine, and which to Rosaline.

Rosaline

Berowne's female counterpart, and anyone who has read the later play, *Much Ado About Nothing*, will see the relationship between Beatrice and Benedick foreshadowed in their clash of wills. Whether or not she will, as Berowne suggests 'do the deed' (III.1.193), we know from Katharine that she is of a 'merry, nimble, stirring spirit' (V.2.16), willing to take on all comers, too hard for Boyet and more than a match for Berowne himself. The penance she devises for him is the severest of all, the most extreme expression of the purgative process to which the play submits unregenerate masculine dominance. Love seems to arouse in her the same ambivalence that we meet in Berowne, and in her later aggressiveness we almost lose sight of her earlier praise of her lover: 'a merrier man,/Within the limit of becoming mirth, I never spent an hour's talk withal' (II.1.66–8).

Plot and structure

The French king's demand for his two hundred thousand crowns is clearly no more than the excuse which brings the ladies to disturb the men's proposed retreat, yet it provides the basic motif of the play. Navarre and his followers attempt to escape from the world, and the

*New Arden edition, p. xv.

world pursues them, with a necessity and reality more pressing than anything contained in their 'little academe'. The Princess's embassy, which threatens their vows as soon as they are made, is followed in due course by Marcade's message of death. The vows with which the play opens are balanced against the penances imposed on the lovers at the close. Though the gradual imposition of the external world of reality on the privileged illusion of the royal park gives the play its shape, it is matched at every step by the collapse of the illusion through its inherent instability. Only fifty lines after Berowne's reminder of the Princess's visit, Dull enters with news of Costard's transgression. Though the events follow each other in an apparently casual manner, Shakespeare is quick to underline the parallels. Act I ends with Armado's soliloquy over his infatuation with Jaquenetta (who thus provides the link with Costard's fall), and Act III concludes with Berowne's confession of love: 'Some men must love my lady, and some Joan' (III.1.200). Though Rosaline is Berowne's Joan, the levelling effect of passion in all ranks of society reaches to Armado's Jaquenetta. The Spaniard's resolution to write sonnets to his mistress, 'For I am for whole volumes in folio' (I.2.175), points forward to the sonnet-reading sequence in Act IV.

The act divisions are made only in the Folio edition, the seamless Quarto edition better matching the flow of this play where no change of scene or scenery need break the web of correspondences. Variety is provided by alternating between the lords and ladies and the characters from the lower ranks of society, present to each other throughout (in, for example, Armado's letters, the first read by the lords, the second by the ladies) and connected by Costard who moves between them, but brought together only in the harmony of the final act. Certainly analogies with music and dance are more suggestive of the organisation of the play than any resemblance to the nineteenth-century novel with its accretion of detail and elaboration of psychological motive. Bobbyann Roesen writes that 'the quality of the whole is very much that of a musical composition, an inexorable movement forward, the appearance and reappearance in the fabric of the play of certain important themes forcing the harmony into a series of coherent resolutions consistent with each other and with the drama as a whole'.*

Shakespeare, however, was primarily a man of the theatre, and self-conscious theatricality is very much a part of the play. Some episodes have a self-contained quality which makes of them 'plays-within-the-play', first and finest the sonnet-reading scene in Act IV. From his hiding place 'in the sky' Berowne invites us to view the antics of his friends like children in 'an old infant play' (IV.3.75-6), until obliged to

*Bobbyann Roesen, 'Love's Labour's Lost', *Shakespeare Quarterly*, IV, 1953, p. 413.

confess his own part in the comedy. We must be conscious of the artificial development of such a scene in order to enjoy it, and it would clearly be absurd to devise some naturalistic plausibility to conceal its symmetry. It can never be a 'slice of life', though from our detached position we recognise the truths about life which go into its making.

The long final act is made up of a whole series of these set-pieces, items offered to entertain the Princess yet reflecting on the actors themselves. The masque of the Muscovites finds an unsympathetic audience unable to discern the sincerity of the men under the exotic artifice of their costumes, because the men themselves can find no true identity from which to speak. When they return to try a different rhetoric, 'russet yeas and honest kersey noes' (V.2.413) in place of 'taffeta phrases' (V.2.406), they have no more success. The pageant of the Worthies continues the theme, with the village schoolmaster masquerading as Judas Maccabaeus, but now the contrast between the lords and ladies in their response to the performance shows how much the men still have to learn before they are worthy of their mistresses. It is yet another of the 'expanding circles of awareness' which have been seen as one of organising principles of the play.

Shakespeare counts on our familiarity with the conventions of comedy to surprise us with his ending. 'Our wooing doth not end like an old play', complains Berowne (V.2.866), but the debate between Hiems and Ver, a revival of the medieval 'conflictus', intended to end the pageant of the Worthies, now serves to complete the whole play, reshaping all that has gone before in a new perspective. Shakespeare's artistry is everywhere apparent even in this early play, in details such as Armado's leave-taking, his vow to Jaquenetta matching the lords' vows to the French ladies, and the last stage direction, 'You that way: we this way', indicating the separation which even the final harmony entails.

Language

So obsessed with language is *Love's Labour's Lost* that more than one commentator has borrowed Moth's words in Act V Scene 1 and described the play itself as 'a great feast of languages' (line 35). Costard's reply—'I marvel thy master hath not eaten thee for a word' (line 37)—characteristically puns on the resemblance between the page's name and the French for word (*mot*). When one character mentions another, it is often to comment on the language he uses, rather than on, for example, his physical appearance. Armado has 'a mint of phrases in his brain' (I.1.164); where another ruler would employ a musician, Navarre 'will use him for (his) minstrelsy' (I.1.175). Indeed, so completely does Armado's language represent his character that his letters give us him as fully as his own person. Berowne's characterisation of the

French lord concludes with 'honey-tongu'd Boyet' (V.2.334), while Nathaniel excuses Dull by explaining that 'he hath never fed of the dainties that are bred in a book' (IV.3.23). The ladies' criticism of the men centres on their verbal wit; in Rosaline's description of him, Berowne's whole activity consists in turning occasions into words, 'so sweet and voluble his discourse' (II.1.76). In their witty exchanges in Act V Scene 2 Katharine mocks Rosaline as 'Fair as a text B in a copy-book' (line 42), and two lines later she herself is 'My red dominical, my golden letter'.

Satire on linguistic extravagance is one of the dishes the feast offers us, in the same spirit that Navarre's friends relish Armado as recreation from their studies. Unfamiliar with the prose style of Lyly or Sidney, we necessarily lose something, though no literary history is needed to savour the absurdity of a letter which opens like this: 'Great deputy, the welkin's vicegerent, and sole dominator of Navarre, my soul's earth's God, and body's fostering patron' (I.1.216–8). As the letter continues, notes in various editions directing us to Gabriel Harvey and Wilson's *Art of Rhetorique* (1553) will allow us to recognise its faithful reproduction of their schematised manner of handling the subject, but the joke throughout depends on the application of high words to low matter, as laughable now as in the 1590s. The same is largely true of the pleasures and difficulties we encounter with Holofernes, though no doubt some knowledge of the pamphlet-wars of the period and the routing of Harvey and the traditional grammarians as the century drew to a close, sharpened the enjoyment of the first audiences. His self-importance involves little selfishness, and as a fellow enthusiast for words Shakespeare handles him gently. Indeed Armado and Holofernes represent extreme forms of failings typical of the other characters.

If the debate between book-learning and real experience, dead languages and living arts, is illustrated by the pedant and Armado, it is central to the whole play, and goes on within Berowne himself. There are no 'natural' characters, except those like Dull 'sensible only in the duller parts' (IV.2.26), and Navarre is right to draw attention to the artificiality of Berowne's attack on the limitations of study: 'How well he's read, to reason against reading!' (I.1.94). The extreme self-consciousness with which the characters speak comes out in the universal fondness for puns, which depend on a separation of words and things, and the compulsion to build up verbal patterns which sacrifice sense to sound and rhythm. If we are examining the themes of the play we may see this as an affectation to be purged, but it is also part of a civilised ideal opposed to the 'barbarism' (I.1.112) Berowne pretends to defend. Verbal exchanges have the aesthetic and dramatic appeal of sport or combat. 'Well bandied both; a set of wit well play'd' (V.2.29) the Princess congratulates her ladies after one such encounter.

The prevalence of rhymed lines, about one half of the total, and of end-stopped lines, was once used to propose *Love's Labour's Lost* as the earliest of Shakespeare's plays, but it is much more likely that he was using them fully conscious of their artificiality, rather than simply reproducing the verbal currency of the day. In Pater's words, 'when he had just become able to stand aside from and estimate the first period of his poetry' (*Appreciations*, 1889).

The love-sonnets of the King and his friends, also published separately, are other examples of this first period, and in their context indicate the Petrarchan affectation which the men must shake off if they are to convince the ladies that their love is genuine. The sonnets are not very good, and deserve Berowne's derision, but his own sonnet has the same clichés: 'Thy eye Jove's lightning bears, thy voice his dreadful thunder' (IV.2.111). Shakespeare could recognise the artificiality of the style, and mock it, though he often contrives to have it both ways, as in his one hundred and thirtieth sonnet, probably written at this same time, which begins 'My mistress' eyes are nothing like the sun'; and ends

'And yet, by heaven, I think my love as rare
As any she belied with false compare.'

After all, the play manages to argue for reality in the face of pretention and artifice, while basing its argument on the highly idealised doctrine which Berowne derives from women's eyes in his Promethean fire speech.

In this speech, the high point of the play, for all its show of logic, we hear the songs of Apollo rather than the words of Mercury, and it triumphs through lyrical intensity rather than rational argument. Shakespeare may commend the 'heart's still rhetoric' (II.1.228), but as a youthful poet he gives it his longest speech. One of Holofernes's Latin tags proclaims that 'With few words a wise man will compass much', but linguistic excess is the rule here. Only with the news of the French king's death, and his daughter's reception of it, do we see real economy, and the effect is all the greater for the contrast:

'The king your father—'
'Dead, for my life!'
'Even so: my tale is told.'

The play

'A pleasant conceited comedy' the Quarto calls it, emphasising the verbal twists and turns that make up the entertainment, but *Love's Labour's Lost* differs from many of the Restoration plays of the late seventeenth century in being more than mere talk. Shakespeare is successful in finding visual equivalents for his humour. The sonnet-reading sequence, which risks repeating the same joke three times over, in allowing us to see the hidden lords and their reactions and Berowne's eventual descent to join them, adds theatrical substance. When Armado's first letter, describing Costard's offence, is read out, we have the aural contrast between the Spaniard's orotund phrases and the swain's monosyllabic interruptions: 'Me? . . . Me? . . . Still me?' but also his actual presence, clownishly cringing before the accusations. Granville-Barker details the choreography which lends grace and movement to the scenes involving lords and ladies, who taken individually as 'character studies' might seem to offer little for our attention.

But if the play is not a comedy of character, it does examine serious themes, the conflicting claims of art and nature, illusion and reality, in no simplistic fashion. The impulse behind the King's opening words is a perennial one, the desire to escape from the flux of time to lasting fame, something to set against 'the huge army of the world's desires' (I.1.10). Ultimately there can be no short cut to eternity, as Berowne recognises more clearly than the others: 'We cannot cross the cause why we were born' (IV.3.214). This world is the only one allowed in the secular perspective of comedy, acceptance of our own affections and discovery of their true nature the only recipe for happiness. Shakespeare gives us all the charm of the golden world, while avoiding the charge of escapism. Death and time are always present, from the 'scythe's keen edge' of the opening speech (I.1.6), through the suffering which love has brought to Katharine's sister, to the death of the King of France and the 'weary beds of people sick' (V.2.814) among whom Berowne is to do penance. In the final songs 'daisies pied and violets blue' will give way in due season to days when 'blood is nipp'd, and ways be foul' (V.2.886, 908).

Even the language, a rich profusion of all the styles available to a young writer in the 1590s, can be viewed as a metaphor for the indecisions and irregularities of the human condition. William C. Carroll sees the central fact about language in *Love's Labour's Lost* as its 'radical instability'.* Perhaps he is right, or at least Berowne in some of his reflections may sound this level of uncertainty, but the play is finally celebratory, in love with something more valuable than anything registered upon brazen tombs, life itself in all its variety.

Though marriage is deferred for a year and a day, the ladies will be waiting, representing a reality impatient of the adolescent excesses of the men, but no less polished, witty and delightful. Love's labour is not fully lost, when undertaken for 'women's sake, by whom we men are men' (IV.3.356).

---

* *The Great Feast of Language*, Princeton University Press, Princeton, 1976, p. 27.

Part 4

Hints for study

Approaching the play

'No play is more discouraging initially' writes E. M. W. Tillyard,*
surely inaccurately if we are lucky enough to see a stage performance.
The bare text is like the libretto for an opera without the music, and our
imagination must supply the sight and sound which count for as much
as story and character. If it were necessary to come to a decision about
the exact nature of the contemporary allusions, whether John Florio or
Gabriel Harvey was the target of a particular shaft, we might well be
discouraged, but none of this need detain us, though it will continue to
interest scholars of the period. The story, such as it is, is clear enough,
the events follow naturally and with predictable consequences. A first
reading will give us all this, and though the extent of the glossary may
be dismaying, the details can be filled in later. Only an audience of
Shakespeare scholars could nowadays hope to catch the point of every
word of Holofernes's 'extemporal epitaph on the death of the deer'
(IV.2.47), but something of the humour of the lame doggerel with its
strenuous alliteration is immediately accessible. We can enjoy the
patterns of language, each 'fit in his place and time' as Berowne argues
(I.1.98), even if the reason for all of them escapes us.

A comedy where so much of the entertainment depends on contrasts
of style and fine linguistic discrimination must present problems if our
command of the language is uncertain, but many of the characters are
themselves in the process of discovering the subtleties of English speech,
and Costard's delight in his two new words needs no dictionary: 'O
sweet gardon! better than remuneration; a'leven-pence farthing better.'
(III.1.164–5).

Nothing about the play invites us to expect documentary realism. We
accept the conventions whereby the King's men no sooner see the ladies
than they fall in love, and no sooner love than express their feelings in
verse. Taffeta masks disguise the ladies so completely that their lovers
are doubly forsworn. We do not doubt that the King will go, as com-
manded, to 'some forlorn and naked hermitage,/Remote from all the
pleasures of the world' (V.2.787–8), even though we have not the
slightest geographical curiosity about such a place. The play established

---

* *Shakespeare's Early Comedies*, Chatto and Windus, London, 1965, p. 137.

its own rules, asking for us only what Coleridge called 'that willing suspension of disbelief for the moment which constitutes poetic faith'.

Yet for all its artificiality, the world of the play is constantly referred back to the world we know, particularly in the deflating comments of the ladies on the extravagant protestations of the men, and in Costard's comic undercutting of the pretensions of the 'little academe', so that we remain both sympathetic participants in the action and detached spectators with all our wits about us.

Repeated readings will make us more conscious of the themes beneath the glittering surface: the debate between art and nature, the relationship between praise and worth, the idea of love and love itself, 'three-pil'd hyperboles' (V.2.407) and 'the heart's still rhetoric' (II.1.228). Passages which seem isolated displays of wit will often prove to come under one of these heads, lending a unity unsuspected from the apparently casual construction of the whole.

Selecting quotations

Works of literature when reduced to generalised summary often seem commonplace and empty. Their power lies in the particular words, and here where the verbal texture is so dense, the detail is everything. Our impression of the characters depends very largely on what others say about them. In the pageant of the Worthies the nobles compete with each other to pin down Holofernes with a phrase: 'The head of a bodkin', 'A death's face in a ring', 'The face of an old Roman coin, scarce seen' (V.2.606,7,8). But we remember him best for his reproach to them: 'This is not generous, not gentle, not humble' (V.2.623). In the same scene, Armado's defence of his beloved Hector sums up the chivalric world in which he lives, investing it with pathos and dignity: 'The sweet war-man is dead and rotten; sweet chucks, beat not the bones of the buried; when he breathed, he was a man' (V.2.653-5). When we call a character to mind, it is often in conjunction with some phrase which seems to encapsulate his essential nature or part in the play. Nathaniel will always be 'a marvellous good neighbour' and 'a very good bowler' (V.2.576,7), though soon dashed.

Berowne's Promethean fire speech, often quoted in these Notes, is an obvious source for the 'doctrine' of the play, though some of Berowne's quieter utterances should be noted too, coming as they sometimes do at the end of scenes in a rhyming couplet, where the break in the action gives us time to reflect:

> 'Well, I will love, write, sigh, pray, sue, and groan:
> Some men must love my lady, and some Joan.' (III.1.199-200)

All the characters are given to sententious expressions, from Costard's rueful 'Such is the simplicity of man to hearken after the flesh' (I.1.215) to the Princess's perception that 'That sport best pleases that doth least know how' (V.2.512), which Berowne is quick to see as a true description of the difference between the failure of their masque and the promised pleasure of the pageant. Such quotations can conveniently be arranged either in relation to the characters or to the themes of the play.

Topics for study

The moral or meaning of the play

What does the title mean? Is the play primarily concerned with poetry and the imagination? Is it an intellectual fantasy, a play of ideas? Is the mocking of male adolescence a major theme? What kind of satire do we find? Is it mere entertainment or something more serious? Does it set up a debate between written and oral speech? Or between true and false wit? Or between book-learning and nature? Does it work towards a redefinition of style in all its aspects: in life, in love, in art?

Plot and structure

Is it deficient in plot and characterisation? How are the scenes with the nobility related to those involving the other ranks? What is the function of the 'plays-within-a-play'? What is the thematic relationship between the pageant of the Worthies and the main plot? Is the unity of the action pictorial rather than dramatic? Is it more like a musical comedy than a play? Does it work through juxtapositions and counterpoint? Does it depend on 'concentric circles of awareness'? Is the basic movement in the play one of transformation? How do the closing songs reflect the play that has gone before?

The characters

Berowne, Holofernes and Armado are perhaps the only characters present in sufficient detail for the traditional 'character study', but you might study the contribution to the action of minor figures such as Costard, Moth or Dull. You might question Muriel Bradbrook's contention that in *Love's Labour's Lost* 'the men have deeper parts for once'.* Or examine the difference between the wit of the ladies and that of the lords. Or compare Berowne and Rosaline, Navarre and the Princess, as loving couples.

* *The Growth and Structure of Elizabethan Comedy*, Chatto and Windus, London, 1951, p. 99.

Language

Does the play deliberately set out to explore the nature of language? Do rhetorical tropes like chiasmus (where elements of a sentence are repeated in inverted order, in the pattern ab:ba) illustrate a disjunctive, antithetical impulse running through the play? Do the numerous puns have any function other than local amusement? What are the differences between Armado's distortions of the common tongue, and those of Holofernes? Is there any norm of correct language in the play? One could examine the transformation of recurrent terms such as 'light', 'fame' and 'worth'.

Given the nature of the play, many of the questions raised can be related to linguistic concerns, and neither these nor those under the three previous headings necessarily have any cut-and-dried answers. We should be familiar with the relevant arguments, some of which have been touched on in Part 3 of these Notes. The works of criticism listed in Part 5 offer other opportunities for joining the critical debate, and other comedies by Shakespeare could be read, particularly *A Midsummer Night's Dream*, *As You Like It*, and *Much Ado About Nothing*.

Essay questions

(*i*) 'A play about courtship which turns out to be a play about love.' Discuss.

(*ii*) 'A sense that language is unreliable is basic to the play's vision.' Do you agree?

(*iii*) How far is the critical, comic testing of love and language the chief purpose of *Love's Labour's Lost*?

(*iv*) Write on the contribution to the action of *either* Moth *or* Costard *or* Dull?

(*v*) 'Fie, painted rhetoric!' How far can we see the play as an attack on rhetoric?

(*vi*) Illustrate the contribution of *either* the sonnet-reading sequence *or* the pageant of the Worthies to the themes of the play.

(*vii*) 'Too picked, too spruce, too affected, too odd'. Attempt a character study of Armado, showing his part in the play.

(*viii*) 'The schoolmaster is exceedingly fantastical; too, too vain'. Describe Holofernes and his role in the play.

(*ix*) 'Berowne is a mouth rather than a formed character.' Discuss.

(*x*) How far can we see the play as advocating a rejection of Art for Life, or Nature?

(*xi*) In what sense do the women constitute the moral centre of *Love's Labour's Lost*?

(*xii*) 'The final songs contain everything in the play.' Discuss.

Writing an essay

Elaborate introductions should be avoided, and examiners are annoyed when candidates ignore the question and simply write down whatever they can remember about the play. It is often helpful to return to the wording of the title from time to time as in the sample essay below to guide the direction of the argument:

(*ix*) 'Berowne is a mouth rather than a formed character'. Discuss.

Berowne's tongue is certainly the source of his strength. Rosaline remembers his 'sweet and voluble' discourse, and his fellow nobles always turn first to him to voice their predicament and proclaim a solution: 'good Berowne, now prove/Our loving lawful, and our faith not torn' (IV.3.280–1). His answer, the Promethean fire speech, finds him the mouthpiece for the 'doctrine' affirming the superiority of the experience of love to the study which Navarre and his followers have mistakenly undertaken.

Berowne, however, has already given us the same argument in the play's opening scene, where his decision to subscribe to the statute in spite of his misgivings shows that his character is indeed unformed. Partly this is a function of his role in the play, that of choric commentator, seen most clearly in the scene where the King and his companions read their sonnets while Berowne looks down from his hiding-place. But we have already heard his own sonnet, and Costard's arrival obliges him to confess that all four are equally forsworn. Berowne's new role of lover forces inconsistency upon him. He who was 'love's whip . . . a domineering pedant o'er the boy' (III.1.169, 172) is now obliged to sue and groan, undergoing all the indignities of his subservience. Yet this vulnerability to change is also an openness to growth and education, even if the first lessons learnt are humbling ones: 'By heaven, I do love, and it hath taught me to rhyme, and to be melancholy' (IV.3.11–13).

Berowne is not a fixed character, like Holofernes and Armado, caught forever in one attitude. His flexibility makes development possible, and the sense of balance towards which the play moves is hinted at from the outset, when he argues against his friends' desire to make themselves old men, wise before their time:

At Christmas I no more desire a rose
Than wish a snow in May's new-fangled shows;
But like of each thing that in season grows. (I.1.105–7)

He is at the centre of the play's paradoxes, seeking for unity and finding it through love. As he tells Rosaline in his sonnet, 'Though to myself forsworn, to thee I'll faithful prove' (IV.2.103). The struggle between affectation and sincerity in which many of the characters are involved, is focused within Berowne himself. He is not a formed character, nor yet a mouth, but a number of contending voices, and as the play progresses he learns to distinguish among them, forsaking 'taffeta phrases' for 'russet yeas and honest kersey noes' (V.2.406, 413). He abandons his role as spokesman—'Speak for yourselves: my wit is at an end' (V.2.430)—and after a 'trick of the old rage' when he mocks the Worthies, comes to recognise the value of 'honest plain words' (V.2.745), though his verbal powers have one more trial to undergo when visiting the speechless sick in the penance which Rosaline imposes.

(*xii*) 'The final songs contain everything in the play'. Discuss.

No thirty-six lines could contain everything that has gone before, and after the verbal fireworks we may be more struck at first sight by the contrast. Yet the songs in Shakespeare's plays usually reflect and refine the action around them, and these are no exception. The 'two learned men' are said to be the composers, but the style is unlike anything we have heard from Holofernes or Nathaniel, a curiously impersonal and universal voice.

Navarre's opening speech opposes 'this present breath' and the march of 'cormorant devouring Time' (I.1.4,5), and his royal park becomes a privileged world where with the ladies' arrival 'revels, dances, masks, and merry hours,/Forerun fair love, strewing her way with flowers' (IV.3.375-6). But the attempt is doomed to failure, he cannot stop the clock, and as Berowne recognises, it would not be desirable if he could:

At Christmas I no more desire a rose
Than wish a snow in May's new-fangled shows. (I.1.105-6)

The ladies, with their greater sense of reality, mock the men just as the cuckoo in Spring mocks masculine complacency.

Death enters the play with the news brought by Marcade. The scene begins to cloud, the penances devised by the ladies are 'too long for a play' (V.2.870), the whole beautiful but artificial world is about to collapse, when the characters return ('Enter all' is the stage direction in the Quarto) for the songs 'in praise of the owl and the cuckoo' (V.1.878-9).

The insistent 'When' introducing each stanza signals the march of time which Navarre could not halt, but now it is the ever-recurring cycle of the seasons. All the actualities of country life, unnoticed among the witty debates of the lords and ladies, come to the fore. Spring gives way to winter, but the owl's merry note is more than a match for the cuckoo's word of fear. 'Greasy Joan' is only one of a number of verbal echoes from earlier in the play, a perennial female claim which neither Armado nor Berowne can escape.

Though the comedy does not end with the traditional marriage, these songs, as C. L. Barber rightly says,* provide an alternative expression of 'the going-on power of life', resolving all conflicts and debates in a larger harmony.

*In his *Shakespeare's Festive Comedy*, Princeton University Press, Princeton, 1959, p. 118.

Part 5

Suggestions for further reading

The text

The text of *Love's Labour's Lost* used in these notes is the New Arden edition, edited by Richard David, Methuen, London, 1956. The New Cambridge edition, edited by John Dover Wilson, Cambridge University Press, Cambridge, 1962, has, like the New Arden edition, useful introductory material.

General works on Shakespeare and his period

BARBER, C. L.: *Shakespeare's Festive Comedy*, Princeton University Press, Princeton, 1959.

BENTLEY, G. E.: *Shakespeare: A Biographical Handbook*, Yale University Press, New Haven, 1961.

BRADBROOK, M. C.: *Shakespeare and Elizabethan Poetry*, Chatto and Windus, London, 1951.

BRADBROOK, M. C.: *The Growth and Structure of Elizabethan Comedy*, Chatto and Windus, London, 1955.

NAGLER, A. M.: *Shakespeare's Stage*, Yale University Press, New Haven, 1958.

ONIONS, C. T.: *A Shakespeare Glossary*, Clarendon Press, Oxford, 1911.

TILLYARD, E. M. W.: *The Elizabethan World Picture*, Chatto and Windus, London, 1943. Brief but useful background for the plays.

TRAVERSI, D. A.: *An Approach to Shakespeare*, Volume I, Hollis and Carter, London, 1968.

Criticism of *Love's Labour's Lost*

CARROLL, WILLIAM C.: *The Great Feast of Language in Love's Labour's Lost*, Princeton University Press, Princeton, 1976.

YATES, FRANCES A.: *A Study of Love's Labour's Lost*, Cambridge University Press, Cambridge, 1936.

Critical essays

ANDERSON, J. J.: 'The Morality of *Love's Labour's Lost*', *Shakespeare Survey*, 24, 1971.

EVANS, MALCOLM: 'Mercury Versus Apollo', *Shakespeare Quarterly*, XXVI, 1975.

GOLDSTIEN, NEAL L.: '*Love's Labour's Lost* and the Renaissance Vision of Love', *Shakespeare Quarterly*, XXV, 1974.

GREENE, THOMAS M.: '*Love's Labour's Lost:* The Grace of Society', *Shakespeare Quarterly*, XXII, 1971.

HENINGER, S. K., JR.: 'The Pattern of *Love's Labour's Lost*', *Shakespeare Studies*, VII, 1974.

HOY, CYRUS: '*Love's Labour's Lost* and the Nature of Comedy', *Shakespeare Quarterly*, XIII, 1962.

HUNT, JOHN D.: 'Grace, Art and the Neglect of Time in *Love's Labour's Lost*', *Shakespearian Comedy*, Stratford-upon-Avon Studies 14, 1972.

HUNTER, ROBERT G.: 'The Function of the Songs at the End of *Love's Labour's Lost*', *Shakespeare Studies*, VII, 1974.

MCLAY, CATHERINE M.: 'The Dialogues of Spring and Winter: A Key to the Unity of *Love's Labour's Lost*', *Shakespeare Quarterly*, XVIII, 1967.

MATTHEWS, WILLIAM: 'Language in *Love's Labour's Lost*', *Essays and Studies*, 1964.

ROESEN, BOBBYANN: '*Love's Labour's Lost*', *Shakespeare Quarterly*, IV, 1953.

WESTLUND, JOSEPH: 'Fancy and Achievement in *Love's Labour's Lost*', *Shakespeare Quarterly*, XVIII, 1967.

There are several books on Shakespeare's plays with sections on *Love's Labour's Lost*, including the following:

ARTHOS, JOHN: *Shakespeare: the Early Writings*, Bowes and Bowes, London, 1972.

BARBER, C. L.: *Shakespeare's Festive Comedy*, Princeton University Press, Princeton, 1959.

BERRY, RALPH: *Shakespeare's Comedies: Explorations in Form*, Princeton University Press, Princeton, 1972.

COLIE, ROSALINE L.: *Shakespeare's Living Art*, Princeton University Press, Princeton, 1974.

GRANVILLE-BARKER, HARLEY: *Prefaces to Shakespeare*, Princeton University Press, Princeton, 1947.

LEGGATT, ALEXANDER: *Shakespeare's Comedy of Love*, Methuen, London, 1974.

PHIALAS, PETER G.: *Shakespeare's Romantic Comedies*, University of North Carolina Press, Chapel Hill, 1966.

TILLYARD, E. M. W.: *Shakespeare's Early Comedies*, Chatto and Windus, London, 1965.

The author of these notes

JOHN SAUNDERS read English at the University of Cambridge and spent two years in Italy before taking a degree in Comparative Literature at the University of Oxford. He has taught at the University of Warwick and is now a Lecturer in English Literature at the University of Newcastle upon Tyne. He has published reviews and translations in various little magazines, and is the author of York Notes on *Measure for Measure*.